OPPORTUNITIES

in

Insurance Careers

HILLSBORO PUBLIC LIBRARIES
Hillsboro, OR
Member of Washington County
COOPERATIVE LIBRARY SERVICES

OPPORTUNITIES

in

Insurance Careers

REVISED EDITION

ROBERT M. SCHRAYER

HILLSBORO PUBLIC LIBRARIES
Hillsboro, OR
Member of Washington County
COOPERATIVE LIBRARY SERVICES

Graw
Hill

New York Chicago San Francisco Lisbon London Madrid Mexico City
Milan New Delhi San Juan Seoul Singapore Sydney Toronto

The *McGraw·Hill* Companies

Library of Congress Cataloging-in-Publication Data

Schrayer, Robert M.
    Opportunities in insurance careers / by Robert M. Schrayer. — Rev. ed.
      p.   cm.
    ISBN 0-07-148207-5 (alk. paper)
    1. Insurance—Vocation guidance.   2. Insurance—Study and teaching—United
States.   3. Insurance—United States—Societies, etc.—Directories.   I. Title.

  HG8051.S355   2007
  368.0023'73—dc22   2007010427

Copyright © 2008 by The McGraw-Hill Companies, Inc. All rights reserved. Printed in the United States of America. Except as permitted under the United States Copyright Act of 1976, no part of this publication may be reproduced or distributed in any form or by any means, or stored in a database or retrieval system, without the prior written permission of the publisher.

1 2 3 4 5 6 7 8 9 10 11 12 13 14 15 16 17 18 19 DOC/DOC 0 9 8 7

ISBN 978-0-07-148207-3 *35856177 11/07*
MHID   0-07-148207-5

Interior design by Rattray Design

McGraw-Hill books are available at special quantity discounts to use as premiums and sales promotions, or for use in corporate training programs. For more information, please write to the Director of Special Sales, Professional Publishing, McGraw-Hill, Two Penn Plaza, New York, NY 10121-2298. Or contact your local bookstore.

HILLSBORO PUBLIC LIBRARIES
Hillsboro, OR
Member of Washington County
COOPERATIVE LIBRARY SERVICES

This book is printed on acid-free paper.

CONTENTS

Foreword

THE UNITED STATES insurance industry has more than 2.3 million people working at diverse and interesting jobs in insurance and reinsurance companies, agencies, and brokers. Insurance premiums in the United States exceed one trillion dollars annually. Insurance is also big business in Canada and other nations.

A major concern of the insurance industry is the decrease of available people to fill positions left vacant by retiring baby boomers and a declining birth rate over the past few years. The United States Department of Labor has identified the financial services industry, which includes insurance, as one of its twelve "high growth" industries.

Initially the workforce shortages are surfacing in the actuarial, claims, and information technology (IT) areas. In addition, other key positions will be impacted in the near future.

Many times when people think about a career in insurance, they immediately think of selling insurance or adjusting claims. These are very rewarding careers; however, they represent only a fraction of the unique skills required to make the insurance process work for individuals and business enterprises.

Insurance or risk management is a process that requires people with a variety of skills in areas such as math, science, communications, engineering, nursing, law, and marketing, to name a few. However, one of the most important attributes an insurance career professional should possess is a strong interest and passion for helping people, whether it is an insurance agent conducting a risk analysis for a young family or a claims specialist responding to the needs of hurricane victims. Their mission is to protect and preserve persons' assets and to come to their aid in time of need.

There is a vast array of opportunities for people in the insurance industry at all educational levels. There are multiple options for those pursuing a career directly out of high school, community college, or four-year university. In addition, many companies and agents offer internships, job shadowing, and scholarships to facilitate the process of learning more about a rewarding career in the insurance industry.

This overview of insurance careers by author Robert Schrayer (and updated by Mark Rowh) offers new insights into opportunities in today's insurance industry. Keep in mind that many of the opportunities may meet your own expectations and interests.

Larry Forrester
CEO and President
Insurance Education Institute

Acknowledgments

The author wishes to express his gratitude to John and Beth Tomkiw for all their research and assistance in assembling this book. Their perseverance and dedication are greatly appreciated.

In addition, the author would like to thank Dick Spencer of the Independent Insurance Agents of Illinois for his timely assistance with research.

Thanks also are extended to the employees and staff of Associated Agencies, Inc., in Chicago for their suggestions and recommendations regarding this book's content.

The editors also express their appreciation to Mark Rowh for his work in updating this edition.

1

IMPORTANCE OF THE
INSURANCE INDUSTRY

THE INSURANCE INDUSTRY is a well-established part of modern life. And even though we live in a time of great change, its importance is not expected to diminish. In fact, with technology racing to the forefront of our society, there will be an even greater need for insurance in the future. With more people and possessions to insure as the future unfolds, the insurance industry will provide a stable career path for those who choose to work in the field.

Just what exactly is insurance? In strictest terms, insurance is defined as a financial arrangement that redistributes the costs of unexpected losses, as well as a contractual agreement in which one party agrees to compensate another party for losses. On the surface, the definition of insurance seems simple enough: someone pays another person or company a predescribed sum to ensure payment against certain damages, conditions, or losses.

Still, insurance is not quite so simple. The very nature of insurance is regulated—by society and governments—and the concept of insurance itself is steeped in complexities. To fully understand the insurance industry, you will want a better understanding of the very roots of insurance—in other words, its history.

Origins of Insurance

Insurance methods have existed in some form or another for thousands of years. Before the development of modern insurance methods, insurance of another sort occurred.

Thousands of years ago, when primitive people first formed social groups, a loose concept of community was formed, and with it came ideas of insurance. Anthropological data reveal that the hunters of these groups worked together to ensure the safety of individuals. When prey was killed, the meat was shared among all members of the group, regardless of who actually captured and killed the prey. In a way, this sharing was the first form of risk spreading—ensuring the group's survival.

Much later in history, systemized insurance methods were created to ensure the livelihoods of a community's citizens.

About 4000 B.C., ingenious Chinese merchants applied the principle of risk spreading to cargo transportation by water. During this period in history naval methods were crude, and many ships capsized in rough waters. To maximize safety, fleets of ships traveling from one harbor to the next often divided their cargoes between ships. If one merchant's ship capsized, only a portion of that merchant's goods was lost at sea. The remaining portions were safe aboard the other vessels in the loosely collected fleet.

Official recognition by legal authorities of the need for insurance occurred in 2500 B.C., when Babylonian King Hammurabi proclaimed there was a need to protect traveling merchants. At the time, Babylon was an acknowledged world leader in commerce, but thieves had taken to robbing caravans along well-traveled routes. A law passed down by Hammurabi provided that a trader would not have to repay a moneylender any monies borrowed to pay for goods in transit if those goods were lost to theft.

This law, in effect, transferred the risk from the borrower to the moneylender. In turn, the moneylender, to protect the investment, often provided patrols to accompany caravans to discourage others from raiding the caravans. The moneylenders further protected profitability by establishing an interest rate for the monies loaned out. The interest was increased in direct proportion to the amount of hazard—or risk—involved in a certain trip. Thus, the first premiums based on risk were established.

Insurance Advancements

As time passed, more advancements were realized. The principle of general average—the spreading of risk to all parties concerned— became firmly established in the Middle Ages, when one merchant's cargo on a ship might be discarded to prevent a ship that was taking on water from sinking. This lightening of the load thus protected the greater investment of all the merchants' cargoes aboard the ship. In return, each merchant would pay a portion of the costs to replace the cargo that was tossed overboard, financially spreading the risks involved and establishing the first method of claims settlement.

In England during the 1600s, great progress was made in moving insurance toward modern-day reality. It was then that Edward Lloyd set up shop in London, offering sailors a respite from the travels of the sea. At Lloyd's establishment, sea captains, merchants, and traders drank tea, ate, arranged seagoing deals, and discussed insurance against financial losses. Soon it became customary for seafarers to go to Lloyd's to arrange insurance for their ships. Thus began Lloyd's of London, perhaps the most famous insurance organization in the world today.

As North America grew, municipalities in both Canada and the United States realized a growing need for insurance. Disasters such as the San Francisco earthquake of 1906, which caused $350 million in damages, and the Chicago Fire in 1871, which caused $168 million in destruction, solidified the thought that formal insurance organizations were needed for towns and private citizens, as well as businesses.

Basics of Insurance Systems

Insurance systems work by redistributing the cost of losses incurred by claims settlements. They do this through the collection of premiums (payments) from all of the participants in the system. In exchange for the premium, the insured (the policyholder) is promised by the insurance provider to be compensated for a loss. Because only a small percentage of those insured suffer losses, the system can redistribute the cost of losses to all members of the system.

Since risks are involved, individuals sponsored by the insurance provider calculate the risks for each policyholder and create a scale of premiums. Therefore, if a policyholder is found to have a greater risk than another policyholder in the system, higher premiums are sought from the policyholder at greater risk. This balances the system by creating fairness for other participants who are not considered such high risks.

In addition to benefiting businesses and individuals, insurance systems benefit society. To begin with, insurance provides stability for families. By easing the hardships suffered by loss, insurance creates a much more harmonious setting for families to thrive in. For instance, repairs to a burned-out home, which are made possible by a monetary settlement for the loss, allow a family to stay in the community.

The business world also benefits from the insurance industry. Insurance aids the planning process of business, since the planner who holds a policy knows that a property loss will not mean financial ruin. Thus, a businessperson can invest more into her or his business to make it thrive, creating more revenue for the company and for the economy as a whole.

Insurance also eases credit transactions, because lenders are more likely to provide funds if they know a debtor's death will not make collection of monies owed impossible. Lenders would also be more apt to make property loans knowing that a disaster would not destroy the financial security upon which their loan is based.

Insurance systems play an important role in creating a fair business system by abolishing the notion of monopolies. Without an insurance system, only the largest companies could survive a disaster or loss. Smaller companies would not have the income or resources to survive fire damage to a shop, for example. However, insurance systems provide assurances that damages would be repaired and losses provided for, thus supporting a free enterprise system where even the smallest business is able to maintain a spot in the marketplace.

Most important, insurance systems bolster the economy by reinvesting the collected premiums into businesses and ventures. They in turn invest in the economy through purchases of materials and services to maintain and grow their businesses.

Because society and the economy are so reliant on insurance systems, certain steps have been taken by the government to ensure that insurance systems remain solvent and law abiding. The insurance industry itself is heavily regulated by local and federal government, with regulations enacted for every aspect of the insurance business. Similarly, the insurance industry polices itself through the licensing and certification of its professionals. Later chapters in this book discuss the regulation of the insurance industry and the certification of professionals within the industry.

Types of Insurance Operators

There are two basic categories of operators in the insurance industry: the insurance company and the insurance agency.

The term *insurance company* typically refers to the insurance business that raises money by investing the premiums obtained from consumers to pay losses of other insured consumers. These consumers, the policyholders, respond directly to the company with their premium commitments, entrusting the company with their security against loss. The company, in turn, hires people to make sure the company's investments make money for the company.

An insurance agency acts as a link between the insurance company and the consumer. The agency seeks out the most advantageous situation for a prospective client, working with insurance companies to find the best insurance package. Once the insurance agency has successfully linked the consumer with the best company for services, the agency receives a commission from the premium the insurance company receives from the consumer. Thus, the employee of the agency acts as the insurance company's representative in the transaction.

Some companies employ their own agents or solicitors, who solicit customers only for that specific company. Within the insurance agency realm, however, agents may service many different companies. Thus, the agency not only represents the consumer but the companies as well.

The term *agent* originally referred to a person who represented an insurance company, while brokers represented consumers, placing business with the companies on the consumer's behalf. In recent years, however, the line between the agent and the broker has blurred, creating a combination of the two—a person representing the consumer and the company. For the purposes of this book, brokers and agents shall be considered synonymous and shall simply be called agents.

An agency's responsibility (and the agent's, for that matter) lies in analyzing the risks that a consumer has. The agency calculates every possible loss that a particular consumer could suffer that might be protected by insurance. Once the agency understands the possibilities for potential loss, an agent then analyzes the ways in which that particular loss could be underwritten by an insurance company at a favorable premium to the consumer. (Underwriting, as applied to insurance, is defined as properly selecting insureds and charging them a rate that fairly reflects the costs and risks of providing insurance protection. Professionals who provide this service are called *underwriters*.)

After assembling these facts, the agency then approaches insurance companies, asking them to quote premiums they would charge to cover the specifications designed by the agent from the analysis of the consumer's risks. Once the agency has obtained a set of quotations, its task lies in analyzing the quotes to determine which insurance company would best protect the assets of the consumer. At this point, the agency also determines the cost effectiveness of the coverage, seeking for the consumer the most comprehensive coverage at the lowest cost.

When a consumer decides to purchase an insurance company's policy, the agent who worked with the consumer then services the consumer or account throughout the policy period. He or she becomes, in effect, the insurance company's representative for the account or the agent for the customer.

Although insurance agencies are defined by their abilities, insurance companies can also be described by the way they are classified and organized.

In the United States, a particular insurance company carries one of three classifications: domestic company, foreign company, or alien company. A domestic company is one that is incorporated within a state where it does business. For example, a company incorporated in California is considered domestic by the state of California. For this reason, a company can be domestic in only one state.

By the same token, a foreign company is an insurance company incorporated in another state within the United States. For example, an insurance company incorporated in Michigan is a foreign company in the state of California.

On the other hand, an alien company is an insurance company that is incorporated in another country. For example, an insurance company incorporated in Mexico is alien to any state within the United States.

How Companies Are Organized

Insurance companies are also defined by how they are organized. Companies can be organized as one of four types: stock companies, mutual companies, Lloyd's organizations, and reciprocal companies.

A stock insurance company is a company in which the initial capital investment is made by subscribers of stock. Business then is conducted by a board of directors elected by the subscribers, or stockholders. Additionally, the distribution of earnings or profits is determined by the elected board of directors. In essence, a stock insurance company is one where stockholders contribute all the capital, pay all the losses, and reap all the profits.

A mutual insurance company is quite the opposite. While the insurance policies offered by a stock insurance company and a mutual insurance company might be similar, there are subtle differences. Members, or insureds, of a mutual insurance company have a dual relationship—they are both the insurer and the insured. They contribute to the payment of losses and are entitled to have payments made in case of a loss. In addition, they are entitled proportionately to the profits of the company.

The policyholders of a mutual insurance company have rights similar to those of stock insurance companies in that they elect company directors who, in turn, hire company officers. Company officers then hire employees who run the company.

Mutual insurance companies can issue policies that are participatory, whereby the policyholder participates in the earnings of the company and receives dividends. These dividends are usually reflected in some sort of rate adjustment.

A Lloyd's insurance company differs from both stock insurance companies and mutual insurance companies in that each member of a Lloyd's organization is an individual insurer. In essence, each member has her or his own capital riding on a predescribed risk. A Lloyd's organization is often called an *insurance pool*.

The fourth type of insurance organization is the reciprocal company. In this system, several individuals may underwrite each other's risks separately. Although this type of company seems similar to the Lloyd's organization, there is one major difference: within a Lloyd's organization, all underwriting members are insurers, but not all members are insureds.

Types of Insurance

Along with the differences in organization, companies can be categorized by the types of insurance they provide. The broadest categories of insurance coverage are life and nonlife insurance. Life insurance relates to all perils associated with human life, while nonlife insurance covers the gamut of all else. Nonlife insurance is further divided into two categories: property insurance and casualty insurance.

Within the property insurance designation, there are several subcategories, including fire, and ocean marine and inland marine insurance.

Fire Insurance

Fire insurance is an important part of an individual's protective coverage, since fires account for more unintended property destruction than any other single peril. Within insurance circles, fire is defined in one of two ways. First, a fire can be friendly in nature. That is, the fire is one that has been deliberately ignited and is intended to be contained within the designated boundaries. For example, a fire within a fireplace can be termed a friendly fire.

On the other hand, a hostile fire is one that is uncontrollable—one that rages beyond designated boundaries. For instance, the fireplace cited in the earlier example can also contain a hostile fire. If a strong downdraft causes the fire to leap from the fireplace, igniting a nearby couch, insurance would cover damages because of the unpredictability of the loss. However, if an item is thrown into the fireplace where a friendly fire is burning, an individual would not be compensated for such a loss. In essence, insurance companies compensate for losses due to hostile fires, and it is up to the insurance professional to decide just when a friendly fire becomes a hostile one and when circumstances warrant payment for losses.

Often, associated perils are included in fire insurance coverage for individuals and businesses, with coverage including natural disasters and circumstances such as windstorms, hail, explosions, and smoke damage. In insurance parlance, these perils are tacked onto fire insurance coverage as extended-coverage endorsements.

Ocean Marine and Inland Marine Insurance

Ocean marine insurance is one of the oldest forms of insurance. Today, ocean marine insurance provides protection against a number of perils, including perils of the sea, war, and theft. This type of all-inclusive protection is known as all-risk insurance, meaning that an insurance company must pay for losses regardless of the cause. Logically, this type of protection is needed for seafaring vessels, since it would be difficult to determine what the cause of a loss would be if a ship sank to the bottom of the ocean.

Inland marine insurance is very similar to ocean marine insurance and was established as an outgrowth of ocean marine insurance. Once cargoes began being transported over inland routes, individuals and merchants saw the additional need to insure goods traveling over land. Inland marine insurance differs from ocean marine insurance in several ways. The most important difference is that insurance companies may place certain requirements and specifications on inland losses and risks, because a company can easily investigate causes of losses that occur over land.

While property insurance covers the land and sea, casualty insurance covers our country's legal system and the workplace. There are three divisions of casualty insurance: liability insurance, workers' compensation, and bonding.

Liability Insurance

Liability means responsibility; legal liability arises out of a general rule of law that an individual is responsible for any loss he or she may cause another to suffer. Liability insurance protects individuals from being sued by people they may have caused to suffer.

Within the law there are three categories of descriptions fitting situations where an individual injures another: civil wrongs done to another, breach of contract, and criminal wrongs. The area of liability insurance is highly complex, uniting several disciplines—including law and statistics—to determine negligence. Often, cases of liability result in lawsuit action taken up before courts. Liability insurance, in these cases, is used to pay court awards on cases regarding negligence.

Workers' Compensation

Like liability insurance, workers' compensation is used as a form of payment when an individual is responsible for another individual's loss. In workers' compensation cases, however, the "individual" responsible is an employer, while the person using the liability system is an employed worker.

For example, if a worker is injured while performing job duties at a workplace, legal liability falls on the employer to provide compensation for the injured employee. Through the use of workers' compensation, an employer may compensate the employee, paying medical and rehabilitative expenses, while providing financial support for the recuperating worker.

Employers often use this form of insurance to ensure that injuries in the workplace do not result in lawsuits. Like the legal liability insurance system, insurance companies providing workers' compensation programs must investigate for possible negligence, determining if a party was at fault in a situation. Such determinations then affect the outcome of provisions and reimbursements. Still, there need not be negligence to collect workers' compensation. It is a statutory system to "insure" workers.

Bonding

Of the three major forms of casualty insurance, bonding is perhaps the most specialized. A bond is an agreement among three parties. One party is the bonding company, while the second is an individual committed to working for the third party.

There are two major branches of bonding: fidelity bonding and surety bonding. In a fidelity bond, the bond company agrees to pay the third party for losses caused by the dishonesty of the second party. In surety bonding, the bonding company (or surety) guarantees the performance of the second party to the third party.

Automobile Insurance

Within the realm of property and casualty insurance, a hybrid exists—automobile insurance. Automobile insurance merges the best aspects of the two forms of nonlife insurance, providing basic security regarding property (the automobile), while ensuring legal liability protection for incidents occurring from the operation of the motor vehicle. Because of the increasing number of automobiles on the roads in America, automobile insurance in recent decades has become a prevalent segment of the overall insurance industry.

Life Insurance

Insurance reduces uncertainty about loss. Although death is not an uncertainty, the time of death is. And when death occurs before an individual has completed a career, it is thought of in insurance terms as a premature death. Life insurance provides protection for the financial loss most often associated with premature death.

Another aspect of life insurance regards the exhaustion of one's income at old age. A policy called an *annuity* establishes a contingency for this sort of situation, providing an individual with a regular income as long as he or she remains alive. Thus, while life insurance guarantees that an individual leaves an estate as financial assistance for her or his dependents (or beneficiaries), an annuity guarantees that an individual cannot outlive an estate.

Health Insurance

Usually placed under the category of life insurance, health insurance provides coverage for risks that are health related. The disruption of a person's normal activities due to illness or injury produces two problems addressed by the insurance world: medical expenses, such as physician and hospital fees, and lost income while an individual is unable to work. Health insurance assists the individual in both instances.

There are three basic types of health insurance coverage: medical expense insurance, major medical insurance, and disability income insurance. Medical expense insurance includes coverage known as basic hospitalization. This type of insurance provides a payment for many services rendered by a physician, as well as most hospital expenses. Thus it protects the insured from financial loss due to medical costs. With most policies, the benefits are paid directly to the provider of the services rendered after bills are submitted by a physician or hospital. This way, the consumer is spared the financial burden of first paying for services and later filing with an insurance provider for reimbursement.

Major medical insurance provides coverage for the cost of serious illnesses. While this type of insurance covers major illnesses, it is often used in conjunction with medical expense insurance to provide more comprehensive coverage. In truth, major medical insurance is designed to provide protection for potentially large medical expenses and often is continued after basic medical expense insurance benefits have been exhausted.

Deductibles are frequently used in major medical insurance. With a deductible, the insured must pay a certain amount of a medical expense before major medical insurance begins to pay medical expenses. In addition, the insurer pays a percentage of the medical expenses, with the insured agreeing to pay the remainder. Typically, the insurer pays 75 to 80 percent of the medical expenses.

Finally, disability income insurance is designed to provide payments to compensate for lost wages due to sickness or in a period of disability. These policies are either short-term or long-term policies, depending on the length of protection offered.

Short-term policies provide a specific number of weeks of coverage, after a brief waiting period. This waiting period is called an *elimination period,* which must elapse before insurance payments can begin. The purpose of the elimination period is to avoid making any payments for minor illnesses. Unlike short-term disability income insurance, long-term disability income insurance provides a number of years of protection, after a much more substantial elimination period.

Some policies include protection for partial disability, providing payments for a person who works part-time while recovering from an illness. In these cases, the payments make up the difference between the individual's part-time wages and the wages he or she would have earned working full-time.

Disability income insurance is available to individuals at different premium rates that are based on the age, gender, and health of the applicant. This type of insurance is also available as an extra cost provision to a life insurance policy. This provision is called a *disability income rider*—a rider being any addition to the policy.

2

TYPES OF INSURANCE CAREERS

THE INSURANCE INDUSTRY offers many solid career options. A variety of positions offer the challenge of diverse duties and new experiences, while providing an attractive source of income for the insurance professional.

The industry itself is booming. And as technology advances, so do specialized insurance fields. New technological fields mean more insurance possibilities and career growth for the right individuals.

For the purposes of this book, available career positions have been broken down into two major categories: agency careers and company careers. In reviewing the various job descriptions, you will see that a number of positions in one category seem similar to positions in the other category. This is intentional, since both types of insurance systems learn and grow from one another. In essence, each system adapts positions to better reflect the needs and wants of the other system. The two systems work with each other continually. Because of this, career positions in the two categories tend to overlap.

At the same time, these positions stress different responsibilities within the context of the respective systems. That is, within the scheme and structure of an insurance company, a position provides different challenges and benefits than would a similar position within an agency.

Of course, the specific features of any company or agency should be considered before assuming that the job descriptions given below can be applied to a particular job opening. With that understanding, the career descriptions in this chapter are meant as a basic guide to the types of responsibilities that can be expected within a position in an agency or company environment.

Agency Careers

Many career possibilities can be found within the agency setting. These range from sales jobs to positions in claims and other areas.

Sales Positions

In a typical insurance agency, several individuals are responsible for maximizing sales production while affording the best possible service to agency clients. In essence, these sales representatives are the backbone of the agency, bringing in clients and servicing existing accounts.

There are several levels of sales personnel within the catchall title of *producer*, with varying degrees of responsibilities.

Account Producer

An account producer seeks out new business, bringing clients to the agency. This individual usually has a fair amount of experience in the insurance industry and ensures that all services provided by the agency are performed properly, following up on all aspects of a client's account.

Account producers need to know intimately the workings of the agency, tracking every aspect of client service. In addition, account producers must have an understanding of their clients' businesses in order to provide the insurance protection that is necessary for successful operations.

Account producers also follow up on client claims, seeking the most equitable situations for their clients. In truth, account producers represent the agency—they are the client's image of the agency.

Account producers typically need a baccalaureate degree and should have prior experience in the insurance industry. The producers need strong verbal and interpersonal skills, given the high amount of client contact they have on a daily basis. They also need strong writing skills to communicate with clients and insurance companies.

Account producers may spend a great deal of their workday in a conservative office environment. As a result, good grooming is essential for all producers, considering the fact that not only are they representatives of the agecny, but the public often sees in them the image of the agency. In truth, to some individuals the producer *is* the agency. Therefore, a neat, well-dressed individual often succeeds at producing new business.

Although the producer often works in the agency's office, he or she may do some traveling while working on new accounts. It isn't uncommon to find a producer making personal calls on a prospective client, whether the call is at the client's business, home, or a mutually agreed-upon setting.

Account Executive

Like the producer, the account executive is responsible for the acquisition of new accounts and servicing existing clients. The account executive tracks an account, making sure that services and functions are performed properly. In essence, the account executive's responsibilities mirror the producer's—with one exception. An account executive generally has less experience than the producer. Therefore, the account executive is usually in a subordinate position to the producer.

The account executive often assumes the producer's full responsibilities when the producer is out of the office. In this way, there is always an individual on hand to service a client's account, affording the client the utmost in service.

An account executive must have a baccalaureate degree with prior experience in the insurance industry, working in some insurance capacity. Account executives must also possess an ability to analyze problems in depth to understand the complexities of a client's needs. The account executive ideally possesses strong verbal, interpersonal, and written communications skills.

Senior Vice President of Sales

Overseeing producers and account executives, the senior vice president of sales encourages active solicitation of business. The senior vice president works with the producers and account executives on current client accounts and actively works on client account renewals. In addition, the senior vice president oversees expenses and determines salaries and fringe benefits of sales producers. The senior vice president typically works in an office but also works in the field, visiting clients to ensure that their accounts are being handled properly.

A bachelor's degree is required of a senior vice president, as well as extensive sales experience as a producer or account executive.

Claims Representative

Within an insurance agency, the claims representative is responsible for the day-to-day duties stemming from property, casualty, workers' compensation, and auto claims, acting as a liaison between the insurance company and clients settling claims. Various levels of claims personnel are also utilized by insurance companies. Thus, the following claims positions described within the context of agency careers also are company positions.

The claims representative takes claims information from clients who experience a loss but can also receive this type of information from producers. Then, the claims representative transfers claim information to the appropriate insurance company department via the telephone or written communication. In addition, the claims representative enters all claims information into the agency's computer or file system in order to maintain a record of all claims for the agency.

Beyond taking such information, the claims representative prepares files on active claims and issues agency checks to the clients when appropriate.

Claims representatives must possess strong verbal, interpersonal, and written communications skills to deal effectively with clients. Typically, the claims representative works in an office and has limited public contact.

The claims representative ideally has a high school (or equivalent) education or an associate degree, although a baccalaureate degree is preferred. In addition, the claims representative should have prior insurance industry experience.

Claims Manager

The claims manager is responsible for setting priorities on tasks and delegating them to the claims representative. In addition, the claims manager reviews losses with producers and processes property, casualty, and auto claims.

The claims manager's responsibilities include reporting all levels of losses for clients to assigned insurance companies, following up with insurance companies for claims payments or additional information, appealing claims on behalf of clients, advising clients on terms of various policies, and managing claims representatives.

The claims manager must possess strong verbal, interpersonal, and written communications skills and must have the ability to organize, set priorities, and delegate tasks. In addition, the claims manager must be able to work without close supervision. Typically, the claims manager works in an office.

Claims managers are expected to have bachelor's degrees. They must also possess prior claims and management experience.

Claims Examiner

The claims examiner is responsible for the processing of group medical, dental, and vision claims for the benefits division of an insurance agency.

The claims examiner's responsibilities include determining appropriate benefit levels in accordance with policy provisions, servicing accounts, and communicating client problems through appropriate lines of communication.

Claims examiners must possess knowledge of medical terminology and must demonstrate strong verbal and written communications skills. Examiners must also be able to organize assignments and set priorities. Typically, the claims examiner works in an office, investigating claims via phone work.

Claims examiners need a high school (or equivalent) education, although a college education is preferred. In addition, prior experience in group insurance is required.

Benefits Claims Manager

The benefits claims manager is responsible for supervising the examination and investigation of claims, while acting as a liaison between claims examiners, clients, and producers.

A benefits claims manager's duties include the training of new personnel, assisting in the redesign of health care plans, acting as a customer relations advocate, and maintaining claim histories of clients.

Benefits claims managers must possess strong written, verbal, and interpersonal communications skills, as well as the ability to manage others in a work environment.

A baccalaureate degree is required to work as a benefits claims manager, as well as prior insurance and management experience.

Marketing Representative

The marketing representative works in all lines of insurance—personal lines, commercial (business) lines, and benefits—quoting and underwriting different types of insurance.

In addition, the marketing representative's duties include completing applications for new orders, processing cancellation notices, preparing billing orders, recommending the proper policy forms to clients, analyzing hypothetical situations, and conducting audits of client insurance policies.

Marketing representatives must possess knowledge of policy forms and coverages. In addition, the representative must have strong financial, mathematical, and writing skills. A baccalaureate degree is required, as well as knowledge of the insurance industry. Prior experience in insurance is also required.

Positions in Insurance Companies

Insurance companies depend on a number of different specialists to carry out their business. The need for qualified persons to fill these roles leads to a wide range of career options.

Actuary

Within the insurance company, the actuary is a highly respected figure. Actuaries deal with the statistical, financial, and mathematical calculations involving the probability of future payments of insurance claims. They, in essence, determine rates for premiums based on the amount of risk involved.

Actuaries study the frequency of hurricanes, fires, tornadoes, thefts, explosions, and other similar disasters. They tabulate the damage caused by such incidents, using the data to estimate financial damages. With this information, they calculate the probability of these types of events occurring again. The actuary then recommends the general range of premium prices that should be charged for insurance to protect clients against these events.

Actuaries must have a keen sense of mathematics and must display financial skills. A baccalaureate degree, preferably in the actuarial sciences or finance, is required of the actuary. Actuaries usually work in an office and have little or no client contact.

Agent

Agents act primarily as salespeople for their company, soliciting clients and new prospects. Once an agent contacts the prospective client, he or she explains the various services of the company and develops insurance plans for the client. Once the client agrees to insurance coverage, the agent acts on behalf of the company in servicing the client.

Agents, for the most part, must aggressively seek out new clients. Companies often place a quota on the number of prospective clients an agent must contact. For instance, a company may ask that agents make thirty calls a week to potential clients. Of these thirty calls, an agent may interview ten interested individuals. In turn, these interviews may actually land only one or two clients. Clearly, an individual seeking a career as an insurance agent must have an optimistic attitude, as well as a gregarious personality.

Although a bachelor's degree is desirable, an interested person with a high school education or associate degree may enter the field as an agent. Often, companies provide training programs for their agents, introducing them to the nuances of the company and its insurance procedures.

Salaries for insurance agents vary. Because the agent works mostly on a commission basis, aggressive agents can command handsome earnings. On the other hand, becoming an insurance agent could be financially ruinous for individuals who do not apply themselves to the rigors of client contact.

Agents often work in an environment that affords them convenient public contact, in communities and metropolitan centers of business. The environment is most often pleasant and can be diverse—agents can work in storefront offices or huge office buildings. They gravitate to where the public is, using their personal traits to gain access to new markets.

Field Representative

A field representative acts as a liaison between the insurance company and the agents who sell the insurance company's policies. Field representatives provide the agent with a vital link to the company, updating procedures and policies for the agent to follow within the course of her or his day-to-day dealings with the public.

Most often, a field representative's responsibilities include making sure agents fully understand developments within the company, advising agents with regard to sales and the servicing of customers and describing new policies. Because of this, the field representative must have an intimate knowledge of the insurance company and the insurance field in general.

Field representatives usually travel a great deal, checking on company agents at various locations. Because of their contact with agents, these representatives must possess keen verbal and interpersonal skills. A baccalaureate degree is often required of field representatives and almost certainly is a requirement for advancement in the field. Many insurance company presidents and top-level executives began their careers as field representatives for a company, learning the various facets of insurance work in the field.

Underwriter

Underwriters most often make decisions on behalf of a company as to the acceptance or rejection of applications for insurance. Working with actuarial data, the underwriter determines whether a potential client is a proper risk, given the type of insurance requested. In addition, the underwriter determines what rates a client should pay for insurance, based on the amount of risk involved with insuring the client.

Because the insurance business is highly competitive, the underwriter's job is crucial to the success of a company. For instance, if an underwriter quotes a premium price that is too low, the company can lose funds over a period of time. On the other hand, if the underwriter quotes too high a price, the company may lose a prospective client to a competitor who offers lower prices for similar coverage. For these reasons, underwriters must possess sound judgment and a strong business sense.

Underwriters work in offices rather than in the field. A bachelor's degree is preferred, and the underwriter should have extensive insurance experience.

Adjuster

Insurance adjusters, also called *claims investigators*, are responsible for determining whether losses are covered by an insurance company. In addition, they determine the financial amount of the losses in order to provide financial payment for losses.

Adjusters can work with many diverse types of claims, ranging from automobile accidents to crop damage, from stolen goods to fire damage. They can also be specialists, working with only one type of claim, such as vehicle damage or flood damage.

Adjusters work in a number of environments. Some adjusters rush to the scenes of disasters and accidents, such as tornadoes and hurricanes. Others work in an office, reviewing claims as they are reported to the company. Because the adjuster has a high amount of contact with the public, he or she must have strong verbal and interpersonal skills. In addition, the adjuster must possess strong written communication skills to convey loss information to company officials and clients.

Although a baccalaureate degree is not required of an adjuster, it is preferred. Because adjusters must be able to explain to policyholders the legal technicalities of insurance contracts, knowledge of law is also useful. In addition, the adjuster must have an extensive knowledge of the insurance field.

Loss Control Specialist

Loss control specialists envision, develop, and implement safety programs that hold accidents to a minimum—thus, controlling losses. These specialists survey work areas and operations, identify hazards, and make recommendations on the elimination of potential hazards.

Loss control specialists work with executives of industrial firms and public institutions, as well as city managers, attempting to correct harmful situations. For this reason, they often travel.

Persons employed as loss control specialists are normally required to have a baccalaureate degree, as well as prior insurance work experience. In addition, specialists should have knowledge of safety procedures, engineering, and occupational health.

Cost Containment Specialist

Cost containment specialists work closely with sales personnel and clients to design specialized health care cost management programs for employee benefits plans. In some cases, insurance agencies have a cost containment specialist on staff, but most often they hire consultants who work with them.

Cost containment specialists work most often in an office but travel to hospitals and other health care provider facilities, setting up hospital cost containment programs and researching new cost containment programs.

Cost containment specialists must have earned a baccalaureate degree. An advanced degree in health care administration is preferred. In addition, cost containment specialists must have an extensive knowledge of health care and employee benefits programs.

Related Careers

In addition to the careers described above, a number of careers in related fields apply to the insurance field. In such cases, these fields may overlap, giving insurance practitioners the chance and challenge to work with individuals who have quite different backgrounds and work experiences. The insurance industry has a need for such individuals and professions, even though such professions don't necessarily work directly in the field of insurance. In essence, these ancillary professions can be called support professions, and the practitioners of these fields can be called support personnel. Without them, the world of insurance would run quite a bit less smoothly.

Following are brief descriptions of some of these professions. Anyone interested in working within the insurance field in a capacity other than as an insurance practitioner should research the various avenues available in pursuing career paths in these professions.

Attorney

Because of the complexity of insurance policies and state regulations, insurance providers often employ attorneys to assist them in proper procedures and the methods of instituting legally sound insurance practices.

Attorneys serve as both advocates and advisors. As advocates, attorneys represent parties in civil cases, such as liability lawsuits, presenting legal arguments in defense of their clients (the insurance provider or the insurance policyholder).

As advisors, attorneys counsel insurance providers as to their legal rights and obligations. They also recommend particular courses of action in business.

Accountant

Accountants prepare, analyze, and verify financial reports for insurance providers, guiding them toward a financially strong business. Insurance providers may have accountants on staff, or they may hire outside consultants to help them with the record keeping of their transactions.

Accountancy personnel also help to maintain accounts payable and accounts receivable departments within insurance agencies and companies. These departments provide up-to-date information regarding financial transactions between policyholders and the insurance provider. Individual accountants coordinate premium billings, as well as act as liaisons between insurance providers and policyholders in matters related to premiums. In addition, they maintain ledger accounts that pertain to premiums.

Human Resources Personnel

Within an insurance company or agency, there is a need to maintain personnel—coordinating the hiring and replacement of workers. Often, this task is delegated to human resources personnel. Their duties include the recruitment of new workers, the administration of employee benefits programs, the administration of wage and salary programs, the administration of payroll programs, the implementation of employee training programs, and the orientation of new employees.

Public Relations Staff

Insurance providers rely on public relations practitioners to maintain a strong and positive image of their business while educating the public as to certain programs or benefits. These practitioners, who are communications specialists, prepare brochures and pamphlets regarding the provider, design presentations, develop newsletters, create speeches for management personnel, and write and place news releases with the media. They may also develop Web pages, audiovisual presentations, and e-mail communications. By doing this, public relations practitioners inform the public of insurance opportunities, creating a sense of awareness about the insurance provider's services.

Nursing and Health Personnel

Insurance companies and agencies often utilize nursing personnel to maintain medical hot lines, which policyholders contact when in need of referrals. These hot lines are also used, in some cases, for the implementation of managed care programs. When employee benefits programs use managed care, employees call these hot lines prior to being admitted to the hospital to determine the extent of insurance coverage. Then the employee can make educated decisions with her or his family physician regarding a hospital stay. In some cases, the hot lines save the employee from unnecessary medical treatment through an assessment of the employee's health and a possible referral for a second medical opinion.

3

EDUCATIONAL OPTIONS

BECAUSE INSURANCE IS a complex industry, some type of education or specialized training is generally necessary to succeed in the field. This may consist of job experience, formal education, or a combination of the two. Many positions within the insurance industry are based on prior experience. In some cases, experience is the best educator.

During the early years of the insurance industry, numerous positions were created through trial and error. For instance, when one person's workload became too difficult to handle, someone else was assigned to various aspects of that individual's functions. Offshoots of job responsibilities created new positions—an adaptation of sorts.

Jobs became more fragmented, with people assuming more specialized roles within an organization as it grew. Indeed, the insurance professional who once handled many aspects of a claim now has individuals assisting her or him. Many of these individuals received their positions—and the additional duties assigned to these positions—through actual work experience.

However, as technology advances and the insurance industry becomes more regulated, the chances that an individual can achieve great success without a systemized education begin to fade. Work experience is an important factor in acceptance to the field, and promotions most often occur to those individuals who persevere, logging in years of experience. But nothing beats a solid education.

If a student feels that work experience is a viable route, here is a word of advice: Seek out an internship opportunity while in school. An internship is a form of education in which an individual actually works part-time (or full-time, depending on the arrangement) at a company, agency, or association in the field, acquiring school credit for the tasks performed while at the firm.

Most often, the internship lasts a school semester and provides valuable experience for the student. The internship's employer, in turn, often gets an eager worker for a semester. A list of associations is featured in Chapter 7.

The student usually must initiate an internship process, contacting an employer in the area to work on ironing out credit details. In addition, the student may want to contact a school counselor to facilitate the process. Some schools even have established internship departments or programs.

Although internships provide valuable experience, today's student must be well-rounded to compete in the career opportunity marketplace. Since the insurance industry is a wider field than, say, accountancy, where the balancing of numbers takes up most of a professional's workday, a broad education is recommended for a career in insurance.

It would help a student to remember that most insurance positions entail several different disciplines. During a given day, an insurance professional may talk with consumers, balance numbers, and work out legalities. Thus, the insurance professional needs service (people) skills, mathematical aptitude, and analytical ability. The only way to get that—and get ahead—is a concentration on a broad range of scholastic subjects.

High School Background

To obtain the proper people skills, a student must interact with a great number of diverse individuals, learning to cope with differing personalities. In a way, the student has done it, unconsciously, for most of her or his life—talking to friends, meeting new people, attending school. Still, interactive skills can be improved through public speaking courses, English courses, and perhaps drama courses. Such studies force the student to make presentations before classmates and instructors and help the student refine speaking skills. At the same time, such courses serve to build a student's self-confidence in communication abilities, an important requirement in the service-oriented world of insurance.

While strong communication skills are important, many types of insurance careers involve mathematics or mathematical principles. Rates, premiums, policies—even risks—are based on mathematics. It would serve the student well to get an early start on what will be a lifetime of working with numbers.

Other subjects are also useful to students who are considering a position in insurance. Social studies provides the student with an understanding of societal needs. History classes make the student keenly aware of the impact certain events have on the economy. Foreign language courses provide a valuable communications tool. In sum, no subjects should be neglected as being outside the realm of this career choice.

Ideally, a student considering a career in insurance should take a course load that includes some or all of the following:

- Three to four units of mathematics
- Three to four units of English
- One unit of public speaking
- One to two units of a common foreign language, such as Spanish or German
- One to two units of social studies
- One to two units of history
- One to two units of computer course work
- Word processing courses

Although this is an ideal situation—to create a well-rounded curriculum—the student should be aware that all courses in some way pertain to life and, in turn, to the selection of a career.

Education After High School

More and more employers are requiring prospective job applicants to have a college or university education. On one level, such an education shows prospective employers the seriousness of the job applicant—a college degree entails hard work and is not undertaken by someone with no sense of personal direction. On another level, such advanced education polishes skills that are learned early on. With the relative scarcity of employment opportunities in current times, college graduates have a definite edge over those individuals who don't have such a formal education.

The advice given to a high school student—taking diverse courses to become a more well-rounded individual—applies to the college student as well. A liberal arts education consisting of a variety of disciplines helps to shape the student's view of herself or himself and of the world. And it affects the attitude taken toward the world later in a career.

Although the student should concentrate on a diverse education, he or she should also take advantage of the range of specialized courses available. For instance, statistical courses fit well with an insurance career, as do courses in economics. Advanced mathematics courses help the student refine computational skills, while writing courses help students learn to organize their thoughts. All these skills are needed to assist the public and carry on business within the insurance realm.

Business courses are also a worthy addition to a college student's course load. The principles expounded upon in these courses can be directly applied within the course of a single day working in the insurance field. Those individuals who have a firm grasp of business principles will also have a greater chance of promotions and success.

In recent years, schools have found that insurance is a scholastic field unto itself. Thus, a number of universities, colleges, and community colleges have established full curricula in insurance.

School of Risk Management, Insurance, and Actuarial Science

A well-known school specializing in insurance is the School of Risk Management, Insurance, and Actuarial Science, which evolved from the 2001 merger of the hundred-year-old College of Insurance and St. John's University. This school now operates as a division of the Tobin College of Business at St. John's University in New York City.

Insurance-related degree programs offered by this school include:

- B.S. in actuarial science
- B.S. major in risk and insurance
- B.S. minor in risk and insurance
- Diploma in risk and insurance
- M.S. in management of risk

Bachelor's level courses include several courses in actuarial science as well as the following:

• **Principles of risk and insurance.** Promotes intuitive understanding of fundamental economic principles of risk and the use of insurance as a systematic approach to transfer and finance risk. Results in students being able to use personal and general business insurance products.

• **Property and liability insurance.** Surveys the liability and property insurance needs of businesses and households and examines the available insurance tools. Results in students being able to use insurance tools to finance common property and liability risks.

• **Life, health, pension, and social insurance.** Surveys market-based and government-based insurance tools for funding premature death, medical care costs, unexpected loss of wealth from catastrophes, and retirement. Results in students being able to finance life, health, and wealth risks using appropriate insurance tools.

• **Risk seminar.** Students collaborate to examine through research more advanced issues in risk management and insurance. Results in students being prepared to apply appropriate research methods to form solutions to risk-related, managerial, or social challenges.

- **Corporate risk management.** Through real-life examples students understand the process of managing risk that organizations face. Results in students being able to collaborate in implementing an appropriate risk management process.
- **Insurance and alternative risk transfer.** Combines insurance and other financial tools into solutions for funding a firm's exposure to risk in ways that create economic value for the firm's owners. Results in students being able to fund jointly the consequences of pure and financial risk.
- **Reinsurance.** Surveys the structure, functions, and products of the reinsurance industry, introduces underwriting and ratemaking for common reinsurance tools, and examines the impact of the reinsurance transaction on insurance firms. Results in students being able to use common reinsurance tools to manage the underwriting risk of property-liability insurance firms.
- **Insurance industry structure and operations.** Analyzes the industrial organization of the evolving insurance and financial services markets and examines the structure and performance of insurance firms. Results in students understanding how market, social, and regulatory forces affect insurance operations.

For more information, contact:

St. John's University
School of Risk Management, Insurance, and Actuarial Science
Manhattan Campus
101 Murray Street
New York, NY 10007
www.stjohns.edu

Many other colleges and universities also offer insurance courses. These include associate degree programs, bachelor's degree programs, graduate programs, and short-term continuing education offerings. Following is an overview of several such programs.

Grant MacEwan College

Canada's Grant MacEwan College offers a program in insurance and risk management through a twelve-month accelerated format. As an accelerated version of a two-year diploma program, it is designed to place qualified students into industry positions as quickly as possible.

Course areas include the following:

- Auto insurance
- Personal and commercial property insurance
- Liability insurance
- Claims
- Risk management
- Underwriting
- Accounting
- Business law
- Economics
- Sales and marketing

Program graduates are prepared to work in a variety of roles in the insurance and risk management industry. This can include working with a wide range of professionals such as accountants, lawyers, medical professionals, emergency personnel, computer specialists, and financial advisors. According to the college, persons with the following qualities are most likely to succeed:

- Problem solving and investigative skills
- Excellent communication skills
- A knack for detail
- A thirst for business and math challenges
- An eye for financial, statistical, and investment data

For more information, contact:

Grant MacEwan College
P.O. Box 1796
Edmonton, AB
Canada T5J 2P2
www.macewan.ca

Daytona Beach Community College

Daytona Beach Community College (DBCC) offers a number of courses to prepare insurance professionals in accordance with state licensing requirements.

DBCC course offerings include the "Life and Health Agents" online course, which is designed for self-motivated students with little time to attend classes and who have some basic computer skills. The course is approved by the Florida Department of Insurance and meets state requirements for those wanting to sit for the state licensing exam. Attendance at a four-hour classroom and exam session is required.

Continuing education courses include:

- Life—Financial Planning
- Agency Errors and Omissions
- General Estate Planning

- Commercial Auto General Liability
- Building Coverage (including dwelling and homeowners insurance)
- Industrial Fire
- Group Life and Health Insurance
- Business Autos (gray areas beyond basics)
- Ethics and the Insurance Producer and Unauthorized Entities
- Commercial Auto
- Life Insurance: Then, Now, and Tomorrow
- Covering the In-Home Business
- Homeowners I and II
- Personal and Business Needs Analysis
- Liability Loss Exposures
- Elements of Life Insurance (intermediate)
- Elements of Health Insurance (intermediate)

For more information, contact:

Daytona Beach Community College
1200 West International Speedway Boulevard
Daytona Beach, FL 32114
www.dbcc.cc.fl.us

CSI Global Education

CSI Global Education offers Canadian students the opportunity to complete the Canadian Insurance Course (CIC), which qualifies students to take the Life License Qualification Program (LLQP) exam (the regulatory and proficiency requirement for life insurance agents in all provinces except Quebec) and become an accredited life and health insurance agent. It helps prepare students who want to acquire insurance expertise as an agent, financial planner, independent broker, or dual-licensed advisor.

Students who complete the CIC are prepared for one or all of four examination/licensing options:

- **Full LLQP (CICF):** qualifies students for the LLQP provincial exam and leads directly to full licensing as a life agent
- **CICA Level A (Restricted Version):** qualifies students for the residual license provincial exam and is a prerequisite for Residual Version CICB Level B
- **CICB Level B (Residual Version):** qualifies "Restricted" license holders to upgrade to fully licensed status by sitting for the Residual License provincial exam
- **Accident and Sickness (CIAS):** qualifies students to take the provincial accident and sickness licensing exam

Those who complete this program learn about the principles of underwriting, contracts, and administration of policies. Specific topics include the following:

- Professional standards
- Common law and contract law
- Taxes
- Needs analysis and risk management
- Underwriting, issues, and claims
- Retirement

- Group insurance products
- Investment products
- Individual disability and accident and sickness insurance products
- Individual life insurance products

CSI's program is offered through an independent study format. Once enrolled, students have one year to complete the course. For more information, contact:

CSI Global Education
200 Wellington Street West, 15th Floor
Toronto, ON
Canada M5V 3G2
www.csi.ca

University of Connecticut

The Center for Continuing Studies at the University of Connecticut is another provider of insurance education. Courses offered help students learn how to advance in the industry, serve clients better, and earn highly respected and recognized professional industry designations. They also show students how to take advantage of the many and diverse career opportunities that the insurance industry offers.

These courses may be of interest to those who wish to work in sales, customer service, underwriting, claims, reinsurance, risk management, and other areas. Offerings include Chartered Property Casualty Underwriter professional designation courses, associate designation programs, the Claims Prelicensing course, and producer workshops.

For more details, contact:

University of Connecticut
Center for Continuing Studies
One Bishop Circle, Unit 4056
Storrs, CT 06269-4056
http://continuingstudies.uconn.edu

Those students who are convinced they would like to enter the insurance field are urged to investigate the possibility of studying toward a degree with emphasis on insurance course work.

For a list of some schools with curricula in insurance or related areas, see Appendix A. This includes colleges and universities offering curricula in the actuarial sciences, which involve the specific application of mathematical and statistical principles to the insurance industry.

4

BECOMING LICENSED

WITH THE WIDELY recognized importance of the insurance industry, state and provincial governments have imposed licensing regulations on the insurance industry and on professionals working
within it. These regulations are imposed for a variety of reasons,
most stemming from a concern for the consumer's welfare.

Along with the need to protect individual citizens and organi
zations that pay for insurance coverage, a major reason the industry is regulated (through the licensing of individuals in insurance
sales) is to maintain certain economic forces. Because the insurance
industry has an effect on the economy and vice versa, measures
must be enacted and monitored to ensure that events within the
industry don't cause wild fluctuations in the economy.

To fully understand the need for regulatory licensing, one must
look for examples at the state, provincial, or local level. For instance,
the bankruptcy of an insurance company through shoddy practices
by unlicensed sales workers can cause great harm to the citizens of
a state or province in more ways than one. First, the premiums col-

lected from individuals and businesses would no longer benefit the economy, because the insurance company couldn't reinvest funds to maintain solvency.

More important, the bankruptcy affects other businesses, many of which cannot function without insurance. If an insurance company becomes bankrupt, smaller businesses, which need insurance to survive in the marketplace, will follow suit. Once these smaller businesses enter bankruptcy, larger businesses, which often need the small businesses for parts, manufactured items, or other services, will be hard pressed to continue doing business. Thus, the elimination of one insurance company eventually causes irreparable harm to the local economy, creating a ripple effect throughout the region.

This type of example can also be applied at the national level, since a nation's economy is comprised of the economies of the states, provinces, and other entities that make up the country as a whole. If businesses in one state or province begin shutting down because of a lack of insurance, the effects would be felt in surrounding states that use the resources of the faltering state. It would actually take only several statewide ripples to create nationwide waves.

There is another important reason regulations are imposed on the insurance industry—licensing is required of individuals working in insurance sales. Because consumers spend a sizable portion of their personal assets over an extended period of time to ensure their own security, great care must be taken to work in the consumer's best interest. Without proper licensing, an unscrupulous individual may take advantage of the consumer's faith in the insurance system. Because the consumer isn't always well versed in the complexities of insurance, the unlicensed sales worker could convince the consumer to invest in unneeded insurance policies. Such actions may spell financial disaster for the consumer.

For these reasons, state and provincial statutes prohibit any person from selling insurance without a license. To maintain licensing, stiff penalties are sometimes enacted by states to ensure that the industry polices itself. For example, Section 492.2 of the Illinois Insurance Law states that it is a misdemeanor for any individual or firm to act as an insurance agent or broker unless licensed. Even when an individual does have a license, he or she may not act as an agent for an insurance company that is not authorized or licensed to do business in the state where the prospective salesperson seeks a license.

Similarly, Section 507.1 of the Illinois Insurance Law states that no company licensed to operate in the state may pay commission to a person who is not licensed, further ensuring that the industry provides an environment for the licensing of salespersons.

Although state and provincial legislation often dictates licensing requirements for the insurance industry, in some cases, particular insurance companies or agencies also create special requirements for its sales force, above and beyond state regulations.

Each state and province has an agency that regulates sales licensing and related matters (see Appendix B for a list of these agencies). In the United States, a commissioner or director generally heads the state department and is either appointed to the position by the governor or is duly elected. All insurance commissioners belong to a separate regulatory body called the National Association of Insurance Commissioners (NAIC). The association meets twice a year to discuss pertinent issues and formulate model bills pertaining to insurance matters. The model bills are often presented before each state legislature simultaneously, in an attempt to achieve uniformly proposed bills on insurance regulations. In effect, the National Association of Insurance Commissioners seeks to create a uniform insurance environment throughout the United States. However, state legislatures in the past have taken the model bills and used them only as frameworks for larger bill packages, tacking on amendments and changes and diminishing the strength of uniformity. In Canada, the individuals who head up provincial regulation are generally known as superintendents, and they belong to a national organization known as the Canadian Council of Insurance Regulators.

Following is a representative look at the licensing requirements for salespersons to give an overview of licensing. Contact your state or provincial insurance department for more information on specific requirements.

Age Requirements

The minimum age for holding an insurance license varies around North America. In some cases, licenses to sell individual types of insurance have different age requirements. Until recently, the minimum age was typically twenty-one. However, changing laws dealing with majority age have resulted in a minimum age requirement of eighteen in some states and provinces.

Application Requirements

Prospective salespersons may be required to submit a written application for a license as well as a producer's bond to guarantee her or his future performance. A producer's bond is obtained from a surety company as a form of guarantee for a salesperson's performance in a prospective insurance company. Producer's bonds are available in predescribed sums, typically starting at $2,500. If a prospective agent will be bringing in a great dollar amount of premiums, a high producer's bond fee is required. Likewise, if a prospective agent brings in small dollar amounts of premiums, a smaller producer's bond is required.

Also, the insurance company that the applicant plans to represent must submit a certificate stating the company is satisfied that the applicant is trustworthy and competent. The insurance company must also state that the applicant will serve as the company's agent upon successful completion of all licensing requirements.

Accredited Course Work Requirements

In some states and provinces, an applicant must pass a prescribed number of accredited insurance courses prior to taking the licensing examination. This requirement is intended to ensure that the applicant is properly prepared for the test. Certification that the applicant for a sales position has completed such course work is an ordinary part of the insurance company's filing responsibility with the state insurance department.

Licensing Examinations

Applicants for a license to sell insurance must successfully pass a licensing examination in their state or province. A fee must be paid before taking the test.

The test format may vary depending on which agency administers it, but all cover the same basic material. For example, the Illinois Licensing Examination is made up of approximately three hundred multiple-choice questions that are broken down into three areas:

1. Life, accident, and health insurance
2. Property and casualty insurance
3. Motor vehicle insurance

Although individuals can take selected sections of the test—opting to take only a motor vehicle insurance licensing examination, for example—most applicants take examinations for every section. This enables them to sell all types of insurance upon successful completion of licensing requirements.

The examinations themselves are broken down into sections, with each area of the examination consisting of a uniform section and a unique section. The uniform section of a particular examination area includes questions that were prepared by the National Association of Insurance Commissioners and are equally applicable to every state. Questions in the unique section of an examination pertain to individual state regulations and subjects that should be covered or given additional emphasis because of special circumstances in that state.

A licensing applicant should be prepared to respond to questions that evaluate three levels of insurance knowledge: recall—definitions of key words and phrases; comprehension—a full understanding of principles; and application—relating principles to problem-solving situations.

Prospective applicants often underestimate the complexity of a licensing examination and try to pass without intensive studies. However, the state licensing examinations cover insurance issues and problems in depth. Following is an example showing the areas touched upon in a licensing examination section for property and casualty insurance agents. In case any of the terms used in this outline are unfamiliar, see the Glossary for a list of terms used in the insurance industry.

Areas Covered in the Property and Casualty Examination

I. Principles of property and casualty insurance
   A. Importance of insurance
   B. Definitions
   C. Characteristics of insurance
      1. Probability
      2. Characteristics of an insurable risk
   D. Classification of companies
   E. Insurance company functions
II. Legal aspects of property and casualty insurance
III. The policy
   A. Parts of the policy including declarations and conditions
   B. Rate making
   C. Coverage
      1. Named peril versus all risk
      2. Items covered by the policy
      3. Losses
   D. Limitations on recovery
      1. Actual cash value and depreciation
      2. Co-insurance
      3. Uses and types of deductibles
      4. Occupancy limitations
      5. Policy limits
      6. Repair or total loss
   E. Notice and proof of loss
      1. Details to be provided
      2. Duty to protect
      3. Cooperation clauses
      4. Appraisal clauses

5. Time limits on lawsuits

6. Claim settlements

IV. Considerations pertaining to types of insurance

   A. Fire insurance

      1. Friendly versus hostile fires

      2. Ignition

      3. Lightning

      4. Consequential loss

   B. Marine insurance

      1. Ocean marine insurance

      2. Inland marine insurance

   C. Liability Insurance

      1. Types of torts

      2. Negligence

      3. Malpractice

      4. Products liability

   D. Personal and commercial packages

      1. Homeowner's policy

      2. Farm owner's policy

      3. Commercial packages

   E. Automobile insurance

      1. Legislation affecting operation

      2. Assigned risk plans

      3. Safe driver plans

      4. Premium rate determination

   F. Theft insurance

   G. Bonds

      1. Fidelity bonds

      2. Bonds for banks

      3. Surety bonds

      4. Contract bonds

   H. Aviation insurance

V. Specific insurance policies and forms

   A. Fire insurance policies (boiler and machinery insurance)

   B. Marine insurance policies

C. Liability insurance policies
D. Personal and commercial package policies
E. Automobile policies
F. Theft insurance policies
   1. Personal theft policies
   2. Business theft policies
   3. Bank theft policies
   4. Forgery insurance policies
G. Bond policies
   1. Commercial fidelity bonds
   2. Three-D policies
   3. Bank bond policies
   4. Surety bond policies
H. Aviation insurance policies
   1. Hull policies
   2. Liability insurance coverage
VI. State and federal government mandated coverage
A. Workers' compensation
B. Federal riot reinsurance
C. Federal flood insurance
D. Federal crime insurance
VII. Government supervision and licensing
A. State and federal regulations
B. Ethical conduct
C. Rate regulation

In Canada, the approach to the licensing examination is very similar but with different sets of questions being asked. For example, in Ontario prospective insurance brokers must take a three-hour exam consisting of ninety multiple-choice questions and one short-answer case study. Each of the multiple-choice questions is worth one mark, and the case study is worth ten marks. The passing score is 75 percent.

The exam content is as follows:

General (47 percent)
RIB act and regulations, registration by-law
Principles and practices in insurance
Theory of insurance
Insurance contract
Meaning and usage of insurance terms
Classes of insurance
Purpose of common policies
Types of insurers

Habitational Lines (18 percent)
Liability:
Comprehensive personal liability
Voluntary medical payments
Voluntary compensation
Voluntary property damage
Contractual liability
Owner's protective liability

Residential coverages:
Fire and extended coverage
Seasonal and secondary residences
Homeowner's package
Tenant's package
Condominium package
Personal floaters
Vacancy permit
Mortgage clauses

Travel Insurance (5 percent)
Policy conditions, limitations, and claim procedures

Automobile (20 percent)
OAP #1—owner's policy form and endorsements
Candidate should be familiar with coverage provided under
    OPF #2—driver's policy
Form and OPF #6—non-owned automobile policy form

Case Study (10 percent)

Certainly, a prospective applicant cannot go into an examination with an indifferent attitude. A position in the insurance field is, in all actuality, a career. When an individual makes a career choice in the insurance industry, personal commitment is definitely a must.

Because of a licensing test's complexity, some states and provinces put a limit on the number of times an applicant can take the test without passing it. If the applicant is unable to pass the exam after the predescribed number of attempts, he or she has to wait until a specified amount of time elapses. In some states, the applicant may be unable to take the test again after a specified number of attempts.

Continuing Education Requirements

Following the successful completion of the licensing examination, many states and provinces require a licensee to continue her or his insurance education at an accredited institution. For example, an Illinois licensee is required to complete twenty-five hours of accredited insurance course work each year for four years after passing.

Temporary Licenses

In some instances, an individual may obtain a temporary license to sell insurance. This authority is typically limited to the following:

1. Individuals who are selling insurance in the presence of a fully licensed agent.

2. Individuals who handle only business renewals and premium collections. This may include a person who is the administrator or executor of a deceased person's estate or the next-of-kin of a disabled agent.

3. Individuals who are hired by a firm and are undergoing a sales training program. In this case, individuals are not allowed to countersign insurance policies. In addition, they must be under continual supervision by the firm they will represent, and they must agree to take the permanent license examination on a scheduled date.

Terminating Licenses

When a license to sell insurance is terminated, there is usually mutual consent between the agent and the insurance company he or she represents. In this scenario, when no violations occur, it is the insurer's responsibility to return the license to the state insurance department.

However, instances do arise that give the insurance department the authority to revoke or suspend the license of any individual. For example, Section 501.1 of the Illinois Insurance Law allows the state to revoke or suspend a person's license after notice and a hearing, if the agent does any of the following:

1. Is found guilty of fraudulent or dishonest practices
2. Misappropriates funds or illegally withholds monies
3. Demonstrates lack of trustworthiness or competence
4. Is convicted of a felony and fails to demonstrate sufficient rehabilitation to warrant public trust

5

GETTING CERTIFIED

EDUCATION AT THE high school level, advanced education, and licensing are all components of the insurance educational process. In addition, the insurance industry provides education advancement opportunities through the certification of industry professionals by specific insurance societies. This practice was established to maintain control over the industry above and beyond state licensing regulations. It ensures professionalism among insurance practitioners by stressing knowledge, skills, and codes of ethics.

Development of Certification

Insurance certification had its beginnings in the first collegiate-level courses offered to individuals interested in insurance work. Before the twentieth century, few colleges and universities were focused on the rapidly expanding insurance field. Therefore, there were hardly any courses in insurance. But in 1904, Dr. S. S. Huebner, an instructor at the Wharton School of Finance and Commerce at the University of Pennsylvania, had the foresight to begin amassing information on the technical and legal aspects of insurance, crafting a collegiate educational program in insurance. From this single university program sprang a host of educational programs for individuals seeking specific knowledge and training in insurance.

Once the roots of certification were established, several organizations sought to establish stringent guidelines for the flourishing insurance field, with the goal of leading insurance professionals toward high standards of conduct.

In 1909 a number of important insurance associations met in Philadelphia, the birthplace of modern insurance methods, to plan an educational program that would be national in scope. These organizations were the Insurance Society of Philadelphia, the Insurance Society of New York, the Fire Insurance Club of Chicago, the Insurance Institute of Hartford, and the Insurance Library Association of Boston. They sought uniformity in the educational instruction of insurance professionals, which in turn would create a uniform insurance system. During this conference, the individual associations banded together to form the Association of Insurance Societies and Institutes of America, the oldest continuously operating national educational program for insurance professionals in the United States.

Once it was formed, the association set about to create an all-encompassing examination of insurance certification. This written examination, held in June 1911, drew thirty-four respondents. It was a humble beginning, considering the many thousands of individuals who apply to take the national examinations today.

Over the years, the association refined testing techniques and took steps toward solidifying testing methods through its permanent incorporation in 1924. With its charter, the association changed its name to the Insurance Institute of America.

Perhaps the most important step toward a systemized level of educational advancement for insurance professionals occurred in 1941, when several organizations met to take the ideas of the Insurance Institute of America one step further. The Independent Insurance Agents of America, the National Board of Fire Underwriters, the National Association of Mutual Insurance Agents, the National Association of Insurance Brokers, the Association of Casualty and Surety Executives, and the American Mutual Insurance Alliance met to plan a professional designation program for insurance.

As a result of that meeting, a national college called the American Institute for Property and Liability Underwriters was created and invested with the power to issue professional designations in insurance. Thus, the certification of insurance professionals was established through the origin of the Chartered Property and Casualty Underwriter (CPCU) designation.

Gaining the Chartered Property and Casualty Underwriter Designation

The Chartered Property and Casualty Underwriter (CPCU) designation reflects a substantial achievement for an insurance professional. It is a badge of honor, so to speak, awarded to individuals who pass a series of complex tests regarding insurance law and procedures. It is so worthwhile that every year a number of people in professions outside the insurance industry take the courses and examination to obtain a proficiency in insurance matters. In truth, the knowledge of the insurance industry and its workings obtained from CPCU courses can benefit a number of professions in the business sector, from accountancy to financial analysis. Therefore, the CPCU examinations are worthwhile to virtually all business professionals.

CPCU course topics cover a wide range of areas, including insurance, risk management, and general business topics. Insurance and risk management principles are applied to the treatment of personal and commercial losses. In addition, insurance policy examples are examined in detail.

Since insurance professionals operate within a business setting, the CPCU curriculum includes courses on economics, accounting, management, and finance to prepare the professional for the possibility of career advancement. The courses also emphasize topics of importance to the field of insurance and risk management.

CPCU courses and subsequent examinations are recommended for experienced insurance professionals who have a strong knowledge of basic practices. They include risk managers, sales professionals, safety professionals, accountants, professors of insurance, attorneys, and other individuals who are in careers requiring a solid understanding of insurance functions.

These courses serve to expand upon one's existing knowledge of the insurance field, using the professional's past experiences as a foundation for advanced theories and practices. For this reason, insurance professionals who consider taking the examination in the future are best advised to continue amassing knowledge while in the field. Clearly, insurance is not a field where one can rest on one's laurels. In truth, the road to certification is paved with experience, dedication, and insight toward advancement.

The CPCU courses are offered in sequences. The best sequence for an individual to take may depend on the amount and type of experience he or she has had in the workplace. Individuals from an insurance agency or company background should first take courses that build on past experiences. For instance, those who work in life insurance should seek out a course that best applies to life insurance situations. Thus, individuals build on successes, using prior knowledge to gain a foothold in course work. Easing into education this way works best for individuals who have been away from educational pursuits for some time, building confidence for their return to the rigors of academics.

The CPCU program consists of eleven courses, of which eight must be successfully completed to earn the CPCU designation. This includes five foundation courses and three selected courses. The five foundation courses are:

- CPCU 510: Foundations of Risk Management, Insurance, and Professionalism
- CPCU 520: Insurance Operations, Regulation, and Statutory Accounting
- CPCU 530: The Legal Environment of Insurance
- CPCU 540: Finance for Risk Management and Insurance Professionals
- CPCU 560: Financial Services Institutions

Other courses lead to a personal or commercial concentration. The commercial concentration (with personal survey) includes the following:

- CPCU 551: Commercial Property Risk Management and Insurance
- CPCU 552: Commercial Liability Risk Management and Insurance

• CPCU 553: Survey of Personal Risk Management, Insurance, and Financial Planning

The personal concentration (with commercial survey) includes these courses:

• CPCU 555: Personal Risk Management and Property Liability Insurance
• CPCU 556: Personal Financial Planning
• CPCU 557: Survey of Commercial Risk Management and Insurance

Following is a description of the topics covered by the various courses:

Required Courses

• CPCU 510: Code of Ethics, Risk, Understanding Risk Management, Risk Assessment, Risk Control, Risk Financing, Financial Services and Insurance Markets, Insurance Mechanism, Insurable Risks, Legal Environment of Insurance, Insurance Policy, Insurance Policy Analysis, and Amounts Payable.
• CPCU 520: Insurance Operations, Regulation of Insurance, Insurance Marketing, Underwriting Property Insurance, Underwriting Liability Insurance, Rate Making, Property Claim Adjusting, Liability Claim Adjusting, Reinsurance, Insurer Financial Statements, Insurer Financial Management, and Insurer Business Strategy and Global Operations
• CPCU 530: U.S. Law and Regulation; Contract Law: Contract Formation, Agreement, Legal Capacity, Consideration, Legal Purpose, Genuine Assent, Form, Interpretation, and Obligations;

Insurance Contract Law; Commercial Law; Property Law; Tort Law: Negligence, Intentional Torts, Products Liability, Environmental Torts, Special Liability, and Litigation Concepts; Agency Law; Insurance Applications of Agency Law; Employment Law; Business Entities; and the International Legal Environment of Insurance

• CPCU 540: Basics of Corporate Finance, Financial Statements, Sources of Additional Financial and Nonfinancial Information, Financial Statement Analysis, Working Capital Management, Time Value of Money, Discounted Cash Flow Valuation, Bonds and Stocks, Operating Environment and Corporate Finance, Insurer Investment Strategies, Insurer Income and Dividend Policy, Insurer Capital: Needs and Sources, Capital Structure of Insurers, Making Capital Investment Decisions, and Mergers and Acquisitions

• CPCU 550: Financial Markets, Federal Reserve, Money Markets, Bond Markets, Stock Markets, Derivative Securities, Banks, Finance Companies, Insurance Companies, Securities Firms and Investment Banks, Regulation of Depository Institutions, Mutual Funds, Pension Funds, and Risks Incurred by Financial Institutions

Commercial Insurance Concentration Courses

• CPCU 551: Property Loss Exposures; Building and Personal Property Coverage; Causes of Loss Forms; Flood, Earthquake, and Specialty Forms; Business Income; Inland Marine and Ocean Cargo; Crime; Equipment Breakdown; Business Owners and Farm Owners; and Surety Bonds

• CPCU 552: Liability Loss Exposures, Liability Risk Control, General Liability Insurance, Business Auto Insurance, Garage and Motor Carrier Insurance, Workers' Compensation and Employers' Liability Loss Exposures, Workers' Compensation and Employers'

Liability Insurance, Management Liability Loss Exposures and Insurance, Professional Liability Loss Exposures and Insurance, Environmental Loss Exposures and Insurance, Aviation Loss Exposures and Insurance, Excess and Umbrella Liability Insurance, and Advanced Risk Financing Techniques

• CPCU 553: Automobile Insurance and Society, Personal Auto Policy, Homeowners Insurance, Other Residential Insurance, Other Personal Property and Liability Insurance, Personal Loss Exposures and Financial Planning, Life Insurance, Health and Disability Insurance, Investment Planning, Planning for Retirement, and Estate Planning

Personal Insurance Concentration Courses

• CPCU 555: Personal Risk Management, Homeowners Insurance, Homeowners Endorsements and Variations, Personal Auto, Recreational Vehicles, Developing Personal Insurance Products, Underwriting Profitability, Pricing, Reunderwriting Personal Insurance Portfolios, and Gaining Efficiencies in Personal Insurance Operations

• CPCU 556: Life Insurance and Social Security; Health, Disability, and Long-Term Care; Basic Investment Principles; Equity and Fixed-Income Investments; Mutual Funds; Asset Allocation; Income Tax Planning; Planning for Retirement; and Estate Planning

• CPCU 557: Commercial Property, Business Income, Commercial Crime and Equipment Breakdown Insurance, Inland and Ocean Marine, Commercial General Liability, Commercial Auto, Business Owners and Farm, Workers' Compensation and Employers' Liability, and Risk Financing

Clearly certification stands for something more than pure educational advancement. It also stands for higher principles—a way of life. Through the rigorous course work and examinations, certification seeks to train the most moral and intelligent professionals possible to serve the public.

Other Forms of Certification

Beyond certification as a CPCU, an individual can become certified in a number of other capacities. Following are brief descriptions of some of these designations.

Associate in Claims (AIC)

The AIC designation is appropriate for experienced insurance adjusters, claims personnel, and those individuals who deal with property losses and liability claims. The program leading to certification as an Associate in Claims outlines principal concepts that involve insurance claims processes and practices, the writing of claims reports, and the reviewing of claims files. The program also includes in-depth discussions of medical terminology and practices—useful information for adjusters working with medical liability cases.

Associate in Management (AIM)

This form of certification is designed for middle management professionals as well as those seeking middle management positions. Programs leading to this designation concentrate on the strengths and weaknesses of existing management practices, human behavior, and systematic decision-making processes. Courses also outline leadership roles in management.

Associate in Risk Management (ARM)

The ARM certification can be of significant value to those responsible for controlling and financing risks of losses suffered by their own company. The designation is also of value to producers who are interested in providing risk management counseling for their individual clients. In addition, underwriters can use the course leading to this designation to sharpen their risk selection.

Programs designed for this designation offer techniques for the identification and evaluation of loss exposures, as well as the analysis of risk control. Financing techniques for exposures, selection of risk management alternatives, and the implementation of risk control and risk-financing techniques are also discussed within the context of ARM courses.

Associate in Underwriting (AU)

Designed for individuals experienced in underwriting and business placement, this form of certification appeals especially to agency and company underwriters and field representatives. Courses are offered leading to this designation that highlight principles of underwriting for property and liability insurance, personal lines insurance, and commercial liability underwriting.

Associate in Loss Control Management (ALCM)

This form of certification is designed for individuals who deal with the selection, design, and implementation of loss control programs. Courses leading to this designation concentrate on the analysis of fundamental principles used in controlling losses to people and property. Courses usually apply these principles to various case situations.

Associate in Premium Auditing (APA)

The APA certification is designed for insurance premium auditors who wish to increase their professional knowledge of property and liability insurance contracts, auditing procedures appropriate to various situations, principles of insurance, insurance accounting, and the premium auditor's relationship with other insurance functions.

Associate in Research and Planning (ARP)

Courses leading to this designation provide an educational foundation for insurance workers in research, planning, and related decision support functions. Courses provide individuals with the opportunity to learn the most up-to-date research and planning methods. In addition, such courses cover basic insurance principles.

Associate in Insurance Accounting and Finance (AIAF)

Aimed at individuals with a professional knowledge of accounting procedures, courses leading to this designation concentrate on the financial operations of insurance entities, providing individuals with the opportunity to master statutory accounting principles, reporting procedures, as well as financial management concepts.

All courses for these designations are available through the Insurance Institute of America. In addition to the educational aspects of certification provided by these courses, each designation allows the individual to waive certain requirements needed for course work toward certification as a CPCU. Thus, individuals can use prior certification as a means of advancement.

Those interested in certification courses are urged to contact the institute at the following address:

Insurance Institute of America
720 Providence Road
Malvern, PA 19355
www.aicpcu.org

The Chartered Life Underwriter Designation

In addition to property and casualty designations, the insurance field offers certification for life insurance practitioners.

Like the CPCU designation, the Chartered Life Underwriter (CLU) designation is thought of as the pinnacle of systemized life insurance education. Individuals seeking the distinction of certification as a Chartered Life Underwriter must pass ten individual examinations, covering such topics as the law and life insurance, estate planning, business planning, pension plans, group and social insurance, accounting principles, and finance theories.

Like the CPCU examinations, the courses offered leading to the CLU designation build on existing knowledge, using it as a framework for expanded study. Again, the individual who is seriously considering career advancement through certification as a Chartered Life Underwriter would be wise to amass knowledge while working in the insurance field. Then the road to certification becomes easier.

Courses leading to CLU certification are available from the American College in Bryn Mawr, Pennsylvania. Interested persons may contact the college as follows:

American College
270 South Bryn Mawr Avenue
Bryn Mawr, PA 19010
www.theamericancollege.edu

Certification in Canada

In Canada the certification process is similar to that followed in the United States. The Insurance Institute of Canada is the primary organization through which professional designations may be earned. Operating through a network of twenty-three affiliated local institutes and chapters, it maintains professional programs, holds qualifying examinations, and elects graduates as Chartered Insurance Professionals (CIP) and Fellow Chartered Insurance Professionals (FCIP).

CIP Designation

The CIP Program, which is the property/casualty insurance industry's professional education program, is recognized throughout Canada and internationally. Participants must complete five mandatory courses, three applied professional courses, and two electives.

Mandatory courses concentrate on essential insurance knowledge, including Principles and Practice of Insurance, the Business of Insurance, Automobile, and Property and Liability. Elective courses concentrate on various specialized aspects of insurance.

Applied professional courses focus on three key career directions within the insurance industry: agent/broker, underwriter, and loss adjuster. Within each area are three course levels designated as essential, advanced, and management.

The steps needed to become a CIP include:

1. Become (and remain) a member of a local insurance institute
2. Complete the appropriate CIP courses for program completion
3. Complete at least one year of full-time employment in the insurance industry
4. Meet the standards of the institute's code of ethics
5. Maintain paid membership in the institute's graduate community, known as the CIP Society

FCIP Designation

Insurance professionals who successfully complete the CIP program may further their education in the institute's fellowship program. Successful completion of this program leads to the designation of Fellow Chartered Insurance Professional (FCIP).

Courses for this program are offered at participating Canadian universities. Participants choose from one of the five majors: management, risk management, claims, underwriting, and broker.

Fellowship students may apply their courses toward completion of an undergraduate or graduate business degree while concurrently completing the fellowship program. For more information about the CIP and FCIP programs, contact:

The Insurance Institute of Canada
18 King Street East, 6th Floor
Toronto, ON
Canada M5C 1C4
www.iic-iac.org

CLU Designation

Those interested in earning the Chartered Life Underwriter designation may consult the CLU Institute, which administers and promotes this designation.

The CLU educational program consists of three specialized courses in life insurance applications, insurance law and taxation, and applied estate planning. For more information, contact:

CLU Institute
350 Bloor St. East, 2nd Floor
Toronto, ON
Canada M4W 3W8
www.cluinstitute.ca

6

EARNING POTENTIAL

ONE OF THE most appealing features of a career in insurance is that it can lead to good pay and benefits. Of course the actual amounts vary widely depending on the type of job performed, the level of one's position, and a number of other factors.

Salaries

According to the U.S. Department of Labor, most wage and salary insurance sales agents earn between $30,000 and $70,000 per year. Some earn less; others pull down more than $100,000 annually.

Insurance agents in Canada earn similar salaries, although figures need to be adjusted to take into account differences in the value of the U.S. and Canadian dollars. For example, an insurance position paying $40,000 annually in the United States might pay something in the order of $47,000 in Canada. Similarly, a salary of $70,000 might equate to Canadian earnings of approximately $82,000.

Independent agents are often paid by commission only. Sales workers who are employees of an agency or an insurance carrier may be paid in salary, salary plus commission, or salary plus bonus. Commission amounts depend on the type and amount of insurance sold and also on whether the transaction is a new policy or a renewal. Bonuses provide another type of income. Typically, they are awarded when agents meet their sales goals or when the employing agency reaches its projected profit level.

Claims adjusters, appraisers, examiners, and investigators earn widely varying salaries. Most earn between $35,900 and $60,000 yearly. Some are paid less, while others exceed $75,000 annually.

For insurance underwriters, typical earnings are $38,000 to $66,000 a year, with some earning more than $86,000.

As with insurance agents, salaries in Canada are comparable once differences in currency have been taken into account.

Salaries and benefits vary not only from one type of job to another but within similar job categories. A number of factors can influence pay levels, including the following:

• **Performance.** For many insurance professionals, earnings are directly related to their sales volume or some other measures of their performance.

• **Educational level.** In many cases, positions requiring a greater level of educational preparation pay higher salaries.

• **Location.** Insurance professionals in large cities tend to make more than those in rural areas, and those in areas with a higher cost of living usually earn higher salaries. For example, housing, food, and other fundamentals tend to cost much more in Los Angeles or Chicago than in rural Alabama or Wyoming. Thus workers in all categories usually demand correspondingly higher or lower salaries and wages.

- **Economic trends.** During times of inflation, salaries and wages tend to go up. When the regional or national economy slows down, on the other hand, raises may be smaller or nonexistent for a while.
- **Skill and experience.** An experienced insurance professional generally earns more than one with little or no experience.
- **Competition.** Competition among companies that employ insurance professionals is often a factor in earning potential. For example, if one major firm raises its salaries, a competing employer may feel compelled to do the same to avoid having employees leave for better paying jobs.

Benefits

Along with salaries or commissions, most employers provide several types of benefits to their employees. Benefits vary from one company to another and are usually more extensive for full-time employees than for part-timers. In some cases, the total amount paid in benefits can be more than 30 percent of the base salary. This can be a significant factor in making a decision about whether to accept a job offer. Such benefits may include the following:

- Health insurance
- Retirement funds
- Paid sick leave
- Paid vacations
- Workers' compensation in case of injury

- Social Security benefits
- Pay for classes or training
- Attendance at conferences
- Transportation expenses
- Computers, cell phones, or other technology support

Employees in some companies enjoy the added benefit of participating in profit-sharing programs, where they may own stock in the company or obtain bonuses based on the company's overall performance. Other possible benefits include extra medical coverage (such as dental or optical insurance), life insurance, performance bonuses, tuition reimbursements, and other benefits.

In considering any employment situation, it is important to learn what benefits are available before making a decision to accept a job. The total package of wages and fringe benefits should be reviewed when considering one job against another, not just earnings alone. It is also important to realize that jobs based on commissions or bonuses include the risk of fluctuating pay levels.

7

PROFESSIONAL ASSOCIATIONS

PROFESSIONAL ASSOCIATIONS CAN sometimes be nothing more than organizations for individuals with like-minded interests to meet and discuss topics of the day. Within the insurance industry, however, professional associations play an important role.

Value of Associations

Professional organizations serve to inform their charter members about current trends within the field, such as changing legislation, new business procedures, and economic developments. Additionally, most professional associations provide seminars and forums to further educate members about the ever-changing field of insurance. The organizations also provide valuable networking contacts—networking being that informal business skill of meeting people in the field for future professional interaction.

Professional organizations can be incredibly helpful to individuals considering careers in the insurance industry. For one, an organization can serve as a networking connection between the interested individual and an insurance company with regard to internship possibilities. Many insurance companies and agencies seek employees who already have knowledge of the insurance business, and internships provide an individual with a fundamental understanding of the day-to-day workings of an agency or company. A successful internship with an insurance company or agency also provides the individual with a ready source of professional references—something that is hard to obtain while enrolled at a university or college. A graduating student with an internship listed on his or her résumé sends out a signal to a prospective employer—one that shows an interviewer that the student is truly interested in the field. Most important, an internship may provide an individual with insight about the insurance profession and may help the student make career decisions based on actual, not textbook, experience.

Beyond internship possibilities, professional associations may provide individuals with interview sources; thus, one may talk directly with people in insurance about career choices. Often, a voice of experience can help an individual make the right decision involving career directions.

Following is a list of professional insurance organizations; each of them includes a brief description as to individual activities and membership. You can contact associations in your area to get a better understanding of the types of career opportunities available where you live. Many of these associations have chapter offices, and they may know of nearby insurance companies and agencies to contact.

Associations of Interest

Advocis
The Financial Advisors Association of Canada
350 Bloor Street East, 2nd Floor
Toronto, ON
Canada M4W 3W8
www.advocis.ca

This association serves Canada's life underwriters. It acts in the interest of life insurance agents and represents their views to government and the public. With more than twelve thousand members in forty-eight chapters, it promotes professionalism among financial advisors, upholds standards of best practice, and supports ongoing continuing education programs, among other activities.

American Academy of Actuaries
1100 17th Street NW, 7th Floor
Washington, DC 20036
www.actuary.org

This association benefits the actuary, who is the individual who applies mathematical probabilities to the design of insurance coverage. The association promotes educational advancement for actuaries, as well as education of the public on actuarial matters. In addition, the organization seeks to maintain high levels of competence for all members, acting as an accreditation body for actuaries. The organization was formed from four distinct associations: the Fraternal Actuarial Association, the Conference of Actuaries in Public Practice, the Casualty Actuarial Society, and the Society of Actuaries. The association provides a speakers bureau of professionals who can lecture before interested groups.

American Association of Dental Consultants
10032 Wind Hill Drive
Greenville, TN 47124
www.aadc.org

This association, which was founded in 1977, was formed by dental insurance consultants to increase awareness in dental insurance plans. The association has a certification program for dental insurance consultants and also holds workshops for educational advancement.

American Association of Insurance Services
1745 South Naperville Road
Wheaton, IL 60187
www.aaisonline.com

This association compiles statistics and creates rates for fire, casualty, multiple line, and inland marine insurance. The association also provides rules that are filed with state insurance departments. The American Association of Insurance Services publishes *Viewpoint*, a quarterly publication.

American Association of Managing General Agents
150 South Warner Road, Suite 156
King of Prussia, PA 19406
www.aanga.org

Founded in 1926, this association provides an educational forum for managing general agents of insurance companies. The association also compiles statistics and provides a speakers' bureau for interested groups. The association also publishes a monthly newsletter that provides information on the role of managing general agents.

American Council of Life Insurers
101 Constitution Avenue
Washington, DC 20001
www.acli.org

Members of the American Council of Life Insurers include legal reserve life insurance companies. The council represents the life insurance business in government and conducts research programs through the compilation of statistics. The council also operates educational and consumer services. In addition, the council has a ten-thousand-volume library of insurance books and publications and publishes a host of material, much of which is available online.

American Hull Insurance Syndicate
30 Broad Street
New York, NY 10004
www.amhull.com

This association acts as a syndicate for the insurance of ocean-going and Great Lakes ships and foreign hulls. The association also acts as a syndicate for the writing of insurance on shipbuilders' risks. The association is designed to assist the development of the American Merchant Marine and the foreign trade and commerce of the United States, offering protection to maritime tradespersons.

American Institute for CPCU
720 Providence Road
Malvern, PA 19355
(215) 644-2100
www.aipcu.org

Established in 1942 and currently affiliated with the Insurance Institute of America, this organization determines the qualifications for professional certification of insurance personnel. The institute also works with universities and colleges with regard to educational standards. Most important, the institute holds examinations and awards certification for the designation of Chartered Property Casualty Underwriter (CPCU), an industry standard. The institute also maintains a vast library of resources on insurance, business, and finance. As part of its services, the institute publishes CPCU course guides and textbooks for insurance professionals.

American Institute of Marine Underwriters
14 Wall Street
New York, NY 10005
www.aimu.org

Founded in 1898, this association of marine insurance companies offers training and educational seminars on marine insurance, as well as the analysis of international agreements affecting marine insurance. The association publishes a daily bulletin.

American Insurance Association
1130 Connecticut Avenue NW, Suite 1000
Washington, DC 20036
www.aiadc.org

This association represents companies that provide property and liability insurance. The association promotes the standing of members through activities, including industry accounting procedures, catastrophe procedures, automobile insurance reform, rating laws, property insurance programs for highway safety, fire prevention, and workers' compensation law reforms. The association also publishes informational bulletins on fire prevention, industrial safety rules, and various laws.

American Nuclear Insurers
95 Glastonbury Boulevard
Glastonbury, CT 06033
www.amnucins.com

Established in 1974, this association consists of insurance companies formed to provide property and liability insurance protection for the nuclear energy industry.

The Americas Association of Cooperative and Mutual Insurance
    Societies
8201 Greensboro Drive, Suite 300
McLean, VA 22102
www.aacmis.org

Founded in 1979, this association supports the cooperative and mutual insurance movement. It helps organizations serve populations who do not have access to insurance coverage.

Associated Risk Managers International
Two Pierce Place
Itasca, IL 60143-3141
www.armiweb.com

This association was formed for independent insurance agencies that provide property and casualty insurance, risk management services, and life and health insurance programs. The association develops and markets specialized insurance and risk management services for trade associations, professional groups, and industry organizations. The association also holds education seminars, maintains a library on insurance and risk management matters, compiles statistics, and operates a speakers' bureau for interested groups.

Association for Advanced Life Underwriting
2901 Telestar Court
Falls Church, VA 22042
www.aalu.org

Founded in 1957, the association caters to advanced life underwriters who specialize in estate analysis, business insurance, pension planning, and employee benefit plans.

Association of Average Adjusters of the United States
79 Palmer Drive
Livingston, NJ 07039-1314
www.averageadjusters.org

Founded in 1879, this association for marine insurance adjusters
maintains an extensive library on marine insurance and topics pertinent to this specialized field.

Canadian Council of Insurance Regulators (CCIR)
5160 Yonge Street, Box 85
Toronto, ON
Canada M2N 6L9
www.ccir-ccrra.org

CCIR is an association of regulators of insurance. Its major purpose is facilitating and promoting an effective regulatory system to
serve the interests of its members.

Canadian Institute of Actuaries
800-150 Metcalfe Street
Ottawa, ON
Canada K2P 1P1
www.actuaries.ca

This national organization promotes high-quality actuarial services. It promotes the advancement of actuarial science through research, sponsors educational programs for members and prospective members, and promotes excellence in professional standards.

Canadian Life and Health Insurance Association
1 Queen Street East, Suite 1700
Toronto, ON
Canada M5C 2X9
www.clhia.ca

This large association, which has been in operation since 1894, serves insurers throughout Canada. It promotes good business practices and serves the needs of insurance companies as well as those of consumers and businesses that deal with insurance companies.

Captive Insurance Companies Association
4248 Park Glen Road
Minneapolis, MN 55416
www.captiveassociation.com

This association of insurance companies was originally formed to provide coverage for sponsor organizations such as manufacturers and retailers. The association provides information to firms trying to solve corporate insurance dilemmas.

Casualty Actuarial Society
4350 North Fairfax Drive, Suite 250
Arlington, VA 22201
www.casact.org

This professional society of insurance actuaries promotes actuarial and statistical sciences in the fields of casualty, fire, and social insurance. It also promotes education in the actuarial sciences and requires all members to pass educational examinations.

Chartered Property and Casualty Underwriters Society
720 Providence Road
Malvern, PA 19355
www.cpusociety.org

Founded in 1944, this professional society is for individuals who have passed ten three-hour examinations by the American Institute for Property and Liability Underwriters and have been awarded CPCU certification. The society promotes education and research in the field of underwriting and sponsors educational seminars, forums, workshops, and research programs.

Conference of Consulting Actuaries
3880 Salem Lake Drive
Long Grove, IL 60047
www.ccactuaries.org

A conference for full-time consulting or governmental actuaries, the association monitors professional conduct and educational requirements of its members.

Consumer Credit Insurance Association
542 South Dearborn, #400
Chicago, IL 60605
www.cciaonline.com

This association was established in 1951 for insurance companies that underwrite consumer credit insurance in the areas of life, accident, health, and property insurance. The association also publishes a monthly newsletter that outlines topics of interest in the field of consumer credit insurance.

Crop Insurance Research Bureau
10800 Farley, Suite 330
Overland Park, KS 66210
www.cropinsurance.org

Established in 1964, this association serves crop insurance companies and organizations related to the crop insurance industry, promoting accuracy in hail loss settlements. The association also promotes the educational efforts of its members through training of crop adjusters and other crop insurance professionals. In addition, the organization provides funding for agricultural university research on crops and crop-adjusting procedures, as well as educational seminars and workshops.

Eastern Claims Conference
P.O. Box 273
Stamford, CT 06906
www.easternclaimsconfeence.com

The conference provides educational seminars to disability examiners, including life, health, and group claim insurance professionals. The educational seminars are designed for those professionals who review medical and disability claims. The conference maintains a speakers' bureau and several informational publications.

GAMA International
2901 Telestar Court
Falls Church, VA 22042
www.gamaweb.com

This association is geared toward life insurance general agents, life insurance managers, assistant agency heads, home office officials, and other insurance professionals who are interested in life insurance field management. The association strives to improve the quality of management, which it does primarily through educational programs, code of ethics practices, and research programs. The association also provides training in management for insurance professionals.

Health Insurance Association of America
601 Pennsylvania Avenue NW
South Building, Suite 700
Washington, DC 20004
www.ahip.org

This association of accident and health insurance firms strives to promote the development of voluntary insurance against loss of income resulting from sickness or accident. It does so through educational forums and research programs. It is an affiliate of the Insurance Institute for Highway Safety.

Highway Loss Data Institute
1005 North Glebe Road, Suite 700
Arlington, VA 22201
www.hdli.org

Established as an association for motor vehicle property and casualty companies, the Highway Loss Data Institute gathers, processes, and provides the public with information and insurance data regarding human and economic losses resulting from highway crashes.

Independent Financial Brokers of Canada
4284 Village Centre Court, Suite 200
Mississauga, ON
Canada L4Z 1S2
www.ifbc.ca

This organization represents independent insurance, mutual fund, and other financial service professionals. It serves as an advocate for members in government and public relations and also provides continuing education opportunities and other benefits.

Independent Insurance Agents of America
127 South Peyton Street
Alexandria, VA 22314
www.independentagent.com

Founded in 1896, this association represents some three hundred thousand agents and their employees in the United States. Organized for insurance sales agencies handling fire and casualty insurance, the Independent Insurance Agents of America provides technical courses for members and publishes handbooks and pamphlets on subjects pertaining to fire and casualty insurance.

Inland Marine Underwriters Association
14 Wall Street, 8th Floor
New York, NY 10005
www.imua.org

This association of insurance companies transacting inland marine insurance provides a forum for members on problems within the industry. The association also makes legislative recommendations with regard to inland marine insurance regulations and provides specialized education courses for members.

Institute for Global Insurance Education (IGIE)
18 King Street East, Suite 600
Toronto, ON
Canada M5C 1C4
www.igie.org

IGIE is an association made up of independent international insurance institutes. The organization's primary purpose is providing professional education to insurance industry professionals.

Insurance Accounting and Systems Association
P.O. Box 51340
Durham, NC 27717
www.iasa.org

This association provides a forum for accountants, actuarial consultants, management consultants, statisticians, and statistical organizations. The association also provides members with research in the field of insurance.

Insurance Bureau of Canada (IBC)
151 Yonge Street, Suite 1900
Toronto, ON
Canada M5C 2W7
www.ibc.ca

This national trade association has represented insurance companies doing business in Canada since 1964. It promotes cooperation among insurers, government, businesses, and others. Member companies provide about 90 percent of the nongovernment general insurance sold in Canada. IBC serves as the trade association for the general insurance industry, playing an active role in promoting the agenda of it members.

Insurance Information Institute
110 William Street
New York, NY 10038
www.iii.org

This association of property and liability insurance companies provides information and educational programs to the media, educational institutions, trade associations, governmental agencies, businesses, and the public on insurance matters and issues. It sponsors seminars and briefings on research and economic topics. In addition, the Insurance Information Institute maintains a library on insurance topics and operates a consumer hotline.

Insurance Institute of America
720 Providence Road
Malvern, PA 19355
www.aicpcu.org

The Insurance Institute of America, which operates in cooperation with the American Institute for CPCU, sponsors educational programs for property and liability insurance workers and conducts examinations for member certification. The association also maintains a vast library of volumes pertaining to insurance topics and related matters, such as finance and economics.

Insurance Institute of Canada
18 King Street East, 6th Floor
Toronto, ON
Canada M5C 1C4
www.iic-iac.org

The Insurance Institute provides educational services for the Canadian property/casualty insurance industry. It maintains uniform educational standards and manages a certification process for insurance professionals.

Insurance Marketing Communication Association
4916 Pt. Fosdick Drive NW
Gig Harbor, WA 98335
www.imcanet.com

Founded in 1923, this association serves the advertising, marketing, sales promotions, and public relations executives of insurance companies.

Insurance Services Office
545 Washington Boulevard
Jersey City, NJ 07310
www.iso.com

This association for property and liability insurance companies provides insurers with statistical, actuarial, policy, and other related services, such as fire protection gradings for municipalities, and fire insurance surveys for specific properties. The Insurance Services Office also acts as an advisory organization on insurance matters and issues. The association publishes a variety of materials, including rate handbooks and policy statements.

International Claim Association
1155 15th Street NW, Suite 500
Washington, DC 20005
www.claim.org

Founded in 1909, this association caters to claims executives and administrators of insurance companies writing life, health, or accident insurance.

Life Insurance Finance Association
4542 Ruffner Street
San Diego, CA 92111
www.lifaorg.org

The Life Insurance Finance Association focuses on consumer advocacy. Open for membership to all qualified persons or entities engaged in the life insurance premium finance industry, it promotes sound and ethical business practices and supports industry regulation efforts. The association also provides information for financial services professionals, life insurance companies, regulators, and consumers about matters of interest related to the life insurance financing industry.

Life Insurers Council
2300 Windy Ridge Parkway
Atlanta, GA 30339
www.loma.org

Founded in 1910, this association (which is affiliated with LOMA) serves multiple line and combination life insurance companies writing life, accident, and sickness insurance.

Life Office Management Association (LOMA)
2300 Windy Ridge Parkway
Atlanta, GA 30339
www.loma.org

Established for life insurance companies, this association provides research, information, and educational activities in the areas of operations and systems, human resources, and financial planning and control. The association administers the FLMI Insurance Education Program, which awards the designation Fellow, Life Management Institute to life insurance company employees who successfully complete a nine-examination program. The association also maintains a library of research materials relating to company operations.

LIMRA International
300 Day Hill Road
Windsor, CT 06095
www.limra.com

Founded in 1945, this worldwide association of insurance and financial services companies conducts market, economic, financial, and human resources research. The association also monitors industry distribution systems and product and service developments. In addition, LIMRA International provides executive and field management development schools and seminars for the insurance industry. The association maintains a library on life insurance marketing and industrial psychology.

Loss Executives Association
c/o Industrial Risk Insurers
85 Woodland Street
Hartford, CT 06102
www.lossexecutivesassoc.org

Founded in 1921, this association was established for loss executives of insurance companies and serves as a liaison between members and independent adjusters.

Mass Marketing Insurance Institute
14 West Third Street
Kansas City, MO 64105
www.mi2.org

This association of independent brokers, carriers, and companies active in mass marketing insurance serves to provide pertinent information on insurance issues to its members.

Million Dollar Round Table
325 West Touhy Avenue
Park Ridge, IL 60068
www.ihs.mdrt.org

Founded in 1927, this association of life insurance agents who sell a predescribed amount of insurance each calendar year conducts several surveys on life insurance.

Mortgage Insurance Companies of America
727 15th Street NW
Washington, DC 20005
www.micanews.com

This association of United States and Canadian mortgage insurance companies provides representation before Congress as well as federal and state regulatory agencies that review housing-related legislation. It also maintains a forum for discussion of industry-wide standards. In addition, the association compiles statistics on topics related to mortgage insurance.

National Alliance of Life Companies
P.O. Box 50053
Sarasota, FL 34232
www.nalc.net

This association of life and health insurance companies conducts specialized education for members and keeps members informed on current legislative matters.

National Association of Crop Insurance Agents
110 North 6th Street
P.O. Box 368
Memphis, TX 79424
www.nacia.org

The association was established for service agents and agencies selling federal all-risk crop insurance to plant farmers. It provides information about insurance coverage on damages resulting from drought, flood, tornado, and other crop disasters.

National Association of Fire Investigators
857 Tallevast Road
Sarasota, FL 34243
www.nafi.org

This association of fire investigators, insurance adjusters, firefighters, attorneys, and members of related professions was established to increase knowledge and improve the skills of persons engaged in the investigation of fires, explosions, and arson. The association also presents awards to members and compiles statistics on fires, fire fatalities, and fire losses. In addition, the association maintains a library on fire-related insurance issues.

National Association of Fraternal Insurance Counsellors
211 Canal Road
Sheboygan, WI 53594
www.nafic.org

This professional organization of sales personnel for fraternal benefit life insurance societies promotes and educates the sales force in fraternal life insurance.

National Association of Health Underwriters
2000 North 14th Street, Suite 450
Arlington, VA 22201
www.nahu.org

Founded in 1930, this association was formed for insurance agencies and individuals engaged in the promotion, sale, and administration of disability income and health insurance. It sponsors advanced health insurance underwriting seminars at universities, as well as other seminars on underwriting topics. The association also testifies before federal and state committees on health insurance legislation. In addition, the association grants certification to qualified underwriters.

National Association of Independent Insurance Adjusters
825 West State Street
Geneva, IL 60134
www.naiia.com

This association caters to claims adjusters and firms operating independently on a fee basis for all insurance companies. It is the originator of an adjusters' educational program administered by the Insurance Institute of America.

National Association of Independent Life Brokerage Agencies
12150 Monument Drive, Suite 125
Fairfax, VA 22033
www.nailba.org

The National Association of Independent Life Brokerage Agencies is comprised of licensed independent life brokerage agencies that represent at least three insurance companies but are not controlled or owned by an underwriting company. The association seeks to further educational plans of members through the application of technological and systems advancements. The association also sponsors research in computer applications to the field, promotion, advertising, and potential profit centers. In addition, the association promotes legislation and regulations that are beneficial to its members and the field in general.

National Association of Insurance and Financial Advisors
P.O. Box 12012
Falls Church, VA 22042-1205
www.naifa.org

Founded in 1890 as the National Association of Life Underwriters, this federation of state and local associations represents insurance professionals, including life insurance agents, general agents, and managers. Associate members of the association include home office officials of life companies, life insurance instructors, and journalists. The association seeks to support and maintain the principles of legal reserve life and health insurance while promoting high ethical standards. The association also sponsors public service programs and an educational series.

National Association of Insurance Women—International
6528 East 101st Street
Tulsa, OK 74133
www.naiw.org

This association for women in the insurance business sponsors educational programs for members and awards a designation of Certified Professional Insurance Woman to those members who pass one of several sets of national examinations.

National Association of Mutual Insurance Companies
3601 Vincennes Road
Indianapolis, IN 46268
www.namic.org

Founded in 1895, this association of mutual fire and casualty insurance companies gathers, compiles, and analyzes information on insurance matters and the reduction of losses. The association also conducts regional workshops and seminars. In addition, the association distributes several publications pertaining to the insurance field.

National Association of Professional Insurance Agents
400 North Washington Street
Alexandria, VA 22314
www.pianet.com

Founded in 1931, this association of independent property and casualty agents sponsors educational programs and seminars annually on aspects of property and casualty insurance. The association also maintains a legislative division in the nation's capital to assist members with pending legislation vital to their interests. In addition, the association compiles statistics, offers consultation and evaluation services, and conducts research. The association maintains a library on a range of insurance issues.

National Association of Public Insurance Adjusters
300 Water Street, Suite 400
Baltimore, MD 21202
www.napia.com

This professional society sponsors seminars and professional education programs for members. In addition, the National Association of Public Insurance Adjusters publishes a variety of materials, including bulletins, brochures, and charts.

National Association of Surety Bond Producers
1828 L Street NW
Washington, DC 20036
www.nasbp.org

Founded in 1942, this association of insurance agents and brokers who write surety bonds provides a forum on pertinent issues for members. The association also publishes a journal on the surety field.

National Council on Compensation Insurance
901 Peninsula Corporate Circle
Boca Raton, FL 33487
www.ncci.com

Founded in 1919, this association is for insurance companies that write workers' compensation insurance. It conducts research, rate making, and statistical programs.

National Council of Self-Insurers
1253 Springfield Avenue
New Providence, NJ 07970
www.natcouncil.com

This council of state associations and individual companies concerned with self-insurance under the workers' compensation laws promotes and protects the interests of self-insurers in legislative matters. The council uses its resources to assist and advise self-insurers with various aspects of insurance implementation.

National Crop Insurance Services
8900 Indian Creek Parkway, Suite 600
Overland Park, KS 66210
www.ag-risk.org

Founded in 1989 as a merger of two other crop insurance associations, this is an association of property insurance companies writing hail and collateral insurance for crop growers. The association develops procedures and educational training for crop insurance adjusters. It also sponsors crop damage research projects at various universities.

National Society of Insurance Premium Auditors
P.O. Box 1896
Columbus, OH 43216-1896
www.nsipa.org

This association caters to insurance company employees who are engaged in field, administrative, or support service policy auditing to determine insurance premiums. The association acts as a forum for the exchange of new ideas in auditing procedures, as well as technical innovations and developments. The association also develops uniform standards for auditing, promotes and conducts research, and holds educational seminars. In conjunction with the Insurance Institute of America, the association sponsors technical education programs leading to member certification as Associate in Premium

Auditing. The association maintains a library of insurance materials, including pamphlets, textbooks, and videotapes.

Organization of Flying Adjusters
416 Augusta Street
Elmore, OH 43416
www.ofainc.org

This association of aircraft insurance adjusters promotes high standards in the processing of insurance claims and seeks to objectively investigate the causes of aviation accidents while promoting air safety. The association also conducts seminars for attorneys, company claims personnel, and manufacturers' representatives on crash investigations and the legal implications involved in aircraft investigations.

Professional Insurance Marketing Association
6300 Ridglea Place, Suite 410
Fort Worth, TX 76116
www.pima-assn.org

The Professional Insurance Marketing Association was established for insurance companies and agencies. It promotes the mass marketing of insurance services while encouraging favorable regulations and legislation for the entire industry. The association establishes codes of ethics for its members and holds seminars to further member education.

Property Casualty Insurers Association of America
2600 South River Road
Des Plaines, IL 60018
www.pciaa.net

This association of property and casualty companies was established in 2004 through the merger of the Alliance of American Insurers and the National Association of Independent Insurers. It currently represents more than one thousand member companies. The association produces more than eighty publications.

Property Loss Research Bureau
3025 Highland Parkway
Downers Grove, IL 60515
www.plrb.org

The bureau, sponsored by mutual and stock insurance companies, holds annual conferences for the loss managers of insurance companies.

Reinsurance Association of America
1301 Pennsylvania Avenue NW, Suite 900
Washington, DC 20004
http://community.reinsurance.org

This association of companies that write property and casualty reinsurance promotes the interests of the reinsurance industry through legislative actions before Congress and state regulatory agencies and commissions. The association also furthers the interests of the industry through the acquisition and dissemination of information and statistics regarding political developments, economic conditions, and technological advancements.

Risk and Insurance Management Society
1065 Avenue of the Americas
New York, NY 10018
www.rims.org

Established for corporate risk and insurance managers, this association provides a forum for members to exchange ideas about the insurance field. The association also sponsors educational seminars, conducts research, and compiles statistics on matters that are pertinent to risk management.

Self-Insurance Institute of America
P.O. Box 1237
Simpsonville, SC 29681
www.siia.org

Actuaries, attorneys, claims adjusters, consultants, insurance companies, corporations, risk managers, and third-party administrators are the backbone of this organization. The institute promotes alternative methods of risk protection as opposed to conventional insurance—that is, promoting the transfer of risk from an insurance company to the individual employer. The Self-Insurance Institute of America seeks to improve the quality of self-insurance plans while protecting the industry from adverse legislation and regulations. The association also provides educational programs for certification and maintains a speakers' bureau to provide information on a number of topics, such as economic conditions, human resources, workers' compensation, and so forth.

Society of Actuaries
475 North Martingale Road
Schaumburg, IL 60173-2226
www.soa.org

Founded in 1949, this organization sponsors a series of examinations leading to a member's designation as a Fellow or Associate in the society. The society also maintains a large library on insurance topics.

Society of Financial Service Professionals
170 Campus Boulevard
Newtown Square, PA 19073
www.asclu.org

This association is a professional society of insurance agents, accountants, attorneys, and other financial specialists who hold professional designations as Chartered Life Underwriter (CLU) or Chartered Financial Consultant (ChFC). The association holds graduate-level educational programs and seminars for members. It also publishes a variety of publications regarding insurance.

Society for Risk Analysis
1313 Dolly Madison Boulevard
McLean, VA 22101
www.sra.org

This association of risk assessment professionals promotes the scientific study of risks posed by technological advancement and serves to collect and disseminate information gathered on risk and risk possibilities.

Surety & Fidelity Association of America
1101 Connecticut Avenue NW
Washington, DC 20036
www.surety.org

Founded in 1908, this association of insurance companies engaged in fidelity, surety, and forgery bond underwriting classifies risks, minimum premiums, and rates. The association also prepares forms, provisions, and riders and prepares statistical data, acting as an information clearinghouse for members.

Water Quality Insurance Syndicate
80 Broad Street
New York, NY 10004
www.wquis.com

This confederation of companies insures vessel owners and operators against pollution liability.

Women in Insurance and Financial Services
6748 Wauconda Drive
Lakespur, CO 80118
www.w-wifs.org

This association of life and health underwriters seeks to advance the life insurance field and informs women members of opportunities in the profession. The association also sponsors educational programs and conducts seminars for members. In addition, the association maintains a speakers' bureau.

8

GETTING STARTED IN INSURANCE

DOES A CAREER in insurance seem to match your interests and abilities? If so, the next step is to make concrete plans for pursuing such a career, and then follow up on them.

Basic Steps

Here are some basic steps you might take to get started in an insurance career:

1. **If you are still in high school, do well in all your courses.** A college-prep curriculum prepares you for study at the next level.
2. **Think beyond high school.** Once you decide what kind of school seems best for you (for example, a community college or a university), fill out admission applications or any other required forms.

3. **If you need financial aid, apply early.** Check out scholarship programs, state aid programs, and the student aid programs sponsored by the federal government.

4. **Once you begin postsecondary studies, go to class, apply yourself, and earn a diploma or degree.** Studies in insurance or business administration or another business-related field will be helpful. Mathematics and similar disciplines can also be useful.

5. **If you prefer an alternative approach, apply for a job with a company that offers its own on-the-job training program or accepts liberal arts graduates or those without a college degree.** Then work diligently to complete the necessary training to work your way up from a lower-level position. For example, you might take a clerical or support job and then use that position to work your way into sales.

6. **Build credentials.** When you gain credentials, either through training or experience, employers will see that you are qualified and motivated to work in insurance.

Finding a Job

After gaining a solid educational background, the next step is to locate the right job. This process requires initiative. It is up to you to find out about job vacancies and then pursue them.

There are a number of possible strategies for identifying job openings. Perhaps the best starting point is to check out online job sites. Examples include Monster.com (www.monster.com), Hot Jobs (www.hotjobs.yahoo.com) and Career Planit (www.jobweb.com).

Along with these general sites, a number of other sites focus specifically on the insurance industry. For example, Insurance-WorkForce.com (www.insuranceworkforce.com) operates as a "niche job board," specializing in addressing the hiring needs of the insurance and financial services industries. It provides both employers and job seekers with a variety of services. Those seeking positions may post résumés, search through job postings, and peruse other information of interest. The site is helpful to those who are currently employed in the insurance industry as well as persons hoping to obtain their first insurance-related job.

Other specialized job sites include:

- Great Insurance Jobs (www.greatinsurancejobs.com)
- Insurance Jobs Board (www.insurancejobsboard.com)
- InsuranceWorks.com (www.insuranceworks.com)

Also, insurance companies and other financial services often post job announcements on their websites. Any firm's human resources office also will provide this information upon request.

Another place to locate job openings is the classified section of any newspaper, although such listings are increasingly being supplemented or replaced by online information. This is particularly true of daily papers serving larger towns and cities.

Still another source of job information is your local employment service or job service office. These offices are supported by state and local governments to provide assistance in locating jobs.

A school or college you have attended also should provide assistance in job searches. To obtain help, contact the school's placement office or one of its career counselors.

Preparing Job Applications

A standard procedure in seeking a job is filling out a written job application. This may be in addition to, or in place of, a standard résumé. If this is required, be sure to do the following:

1. Take your time in filling out the form.

2. Answer all questions completely and honestly.

3. Be as neat as possible. If time and circumstances allow, type the application or prepare it using word processing software. If this is not possible, write neatly and legibly. Use a pen, not a pencil, and remember that you are trying to make a good impression.

4. Check your work closely for errors in spelling or grammar.

5. Have a résumé ready. Prepare a neatly word-processed résumé in advance, and attach it to applications or use it instead of application forms, if allowed.

6. Get your references on board. For persons you list as references, make certain you have contacted them in advance both to get their permission for such usage and to make sure they will be prepared to give you a positive recommendation.

If you are posting an online application or résumé, adapt these guidelines to the electronic medium. Be sure to use concise wording and run a spell-check program.

Succeeding in Interviews

A completed application may be followed by a job interview. It is here that most jobs are won or lost, with the written application serving only to get you to this stage. To do your best in interviews, take measures such as these:

1. Be sure to arrive on time. Lateness only makes a bad impression, and it may cost you the job.

2. Avoid being too eager. Even if you think you need the job badly, try not to show it. A calm, professional manner works best. Act interested, but not desperate.

3. **Dress neatly.** Appearances really do count. Make sure you wear clean, neat clothes appropriate for a business setting.

4. **Make certain to engage in a two-way conversation.** Even though it is the interviewer's job to ask most of the questions, ask some questions of your own. These should dwell on the nature of the job, not on issues such as wages and benefits, which can be discussed in more detail if you are offered the job. Show that you are interested and capable of asking intelligent questions.

Will your interview lead to a job? Only the actual experience in any given situation will tell. Usually it takes a combination of ability, potential, and good luck. But remember, it only takes one success! Once you land that job, you can begin working in the insurance industry and enjoy the potential such a move holds for a challenging career in an exciting field.

Appendix A

Schools Offering
Insurance-Related Programs

FOLLOWING ARE SOME of the postsecondary institutions in the United States and Canada that offer insurance-related programs. For more information, contact any of the schools listed. You can also contact other schools or your state or provincial higher education agency to identify additional educational options.

Appalachian State University
Boone, NC 28608
www.appstate.edu

Arizona State University
Tempe, AZ 85287
www.asu.edu

Bowling Green State University
Bowling Green, OH 43403
www.bgsu.edu

Casper College
125 College Dr.
Casper, WY 82601
www.caspercollege.edu

Centennial College
P.O. Box 631, Station A
Toronto (Scarborough), ON
Canada M1K 5E9
www.centennialcollege.ca

Central Texas College
US Highway 190 West
Killeen, TX 76540
www.ctcd.edu

City University of New York
Baruch College
17 Lexington Ave.
New York, NY 10010
www.baruch.cuny.edu

City University of New York
Queensborough Community College
Springfield Blvd. and Fifty-Sixth Ave.
Bayside, NY 11364
www.qcc.cuny.edu

Clarion University of Pennsylvania
Clarion, PA 16214
www.clarion.edu

CSI Global Education
200 Wellington St. West, 15th Fl.
Toronto, ON
Canada M5V 3G2
www.csi.ca

Drake University
Twenty-Fifth St. and University Ave.
Des Moines, IA 50311
www.drake.edu

Eastern Kentucky University
Richmond, KY 40475-3102
www.eke.edu

Florida State University
Tallahassee, FL 32306
www.fsu.edu

Gadsden State Community College
1001 Wallace Dr.
Gadsden, AL 35902
www.gadsdenstate.edu

Grant MacEwan College
P.O. Box 1796
Edmonton, AB
Canada T5J 2P2
www.macewan.ca

Husson College
1 College Cir.
Bangor, ME 04401
www.husson.edu

Hutchinson Community College
1300 N. Plum St.
Hutchinson, KS 67501
www.hutchcc.edu

Illinois Wesleyan University
P.O. Box 2900
Bloomington, IL 61702
www.iwu.edu

Indiana University at Bloomington
Bloomington, IN 47405
www.iub.edu

Michigan State University
East Lansing, MI 48824
www.msu.edu

MidAmerica Nazarene University
2030 E. College Way
Olathe, KS 66062
www.mnu.edu

Middle Tennessee State University
Murfreesboro, TN 37132
www.mtsu.edu

Minnesota State University–Mankato
South Rd. and Ellis Ave.
Mankato, MN 56002
www.mnsu.edu

Mohawk Valley Community College
1101 Sherman Dr.
Utica, NY 13501
www.mvcc.edu

New Mexico State University
Las Cruces, NM 88003
www.nmsu.edu

North Dakota State University
Fargo, ND 58102
www.ndsu.edu

Oklahoma State University
Stillwater, OK 74078
www.okstate.edu

Olivet College
Olivet, MI 49076
www.olivetcollege.edu

Pennsylvania State University
201 Old Main
University Park, PA 16802
www.psu.edu

St. John's University
School of Risk Management, Insurance, and Actuarial Science
Manhattan Campus
101 Murray St.
New York, NY 10007
www.stjohns.edu

St. Mary's University
1 Camino Santa Maria
San Antonio, TX 78228
www.stmarytx.edu

Thomas Edison State College
101 W. State St.
Trenton, NJ 08608
www.tesc.edu

University of Alabama
Tuscaloosa, AL 35401
www.ua.edu

University of Arkansas
Fayetteville, AR 72701
www.uark.edu

University of Cincinnati
Cincinnati, OH 45221
www.uc.edu

University of Connecticut
Storrs, CT 06269
www.uconn.edu

University of Florida
Gainesville, FL 32611
www.ufl.edu

University of Hartford
200 Bloomfield Ave.
West Hartford, CT 06117
www.hartford.edu

University of Iowa
Iowa City, IA 52242
www.uiow.edu

Université Laval
Québec
Canada, G1K 7P4
www.ulaval.ca

The University of Memphis
Memphis, TN 38152
www.memphis.edu

University of Nevada–Las Vegas
4505 S. Maryland Pkwy.
Las Vegas, NV 89154
www.unlv.edu

University of Northern Colorado
Greeley, CO 80639
www.unco.edu

University of Rhode Island
Kingston, RI 02881
www.uri.edu

University of South Carolina
Columbia, SC 29208
www.sc.edu

University of Southern Mississippi
Southern Station Box 5167
Hattiesburg, MS 39406
www.usm.edu

University of Waterloo
200 University Ave. West
Waterloo, ON
Canada N2L 3G1
www.uwaterloo.ca

Washington State University
2580 NE Grimes Way
Pullman, WA 99164
www.wsu.edu

Wilfrid Laurier University
75 University Ave. West
Waterloo, ON
Canada, N2L 3C5
www.wlu.ca

In addition to the schools offering insurance course work for students, a number of colleges and universities offer curricula in actuarial sciences. The actuarial sciences involve the specific application of mathematical and statistical principles to rate making within insurance. Following is a list of some schools offering curricula in the actuarial sciences.

Ball State University
Muncie, IN 47306
www.bus.edu

Butler University
Forty-Sixth at Sunset Ave.
Indianapolis, IN 46208
www.butler.edu

Concordia University
1455 de Maisonneuve Blvd. W.
Montreal, QC
Canada, H3G 1M8
www.concordia.ca

Drake University
Twenty-Fifth St. and University Ave.
Des Moines, IA 50311
www.drake.edu

Georgia State University
University Plaza
Atlanta, GA 30303-3082
www.gsu.edu

Lebanon Valley College
Annville, PA 17003-0501
www.lvc.edu

Maryville College
Maryville, TN 37804
www.maryvillecollege.edu

Ohio State University
Columbus, OH 43210-1358
www.osu.edu

Oregon State University
Corvallis, OR 97331
www.oregonstate.edu

HILLSBORO PUBLIC LIBRARIES
Hillsboro, OR
Member of Washington County
COOPERATIVE LIBRARY SERVICES

Pennsylvania State University
201 Old Main
University Park, PA 16802
www.psu.edu

Roosevelt University
430 S. Michigan Ave.
Chicago, IL 60605-1394
www.roosevelt.edu

State University of New York–Buffalo
Buffalo, NY 14214
www.buffalo.edu

Temple University
Philadelphia, PA 19122
www.temple.edu

University of Alberta
Edmonton, AB
Canada T6G 2G1
www.ualberta.ca

University of Cincinnati
Cincinnati, OH 45221
www.uc.edu

University of Connecticut
Storrs, CT 06269
www.uconn.edu

HILLSBORO PUBLIC LIBRARIES
Hillsboro, OR
Member of Washington County
COOPERATIVE LIBRARY SERVICES

University of Hartford
200 Bloomfield Ave.
West Hartford, CT 06117-0395
www.hartford.edu

University of Iowa
Iowa City, IA 52242
www.uiowa.edu

University of Michigan
Ann Arbor, MI 48109
www.umich.edu

University of Minnesota–Twin Cities
Minneapolis, MN 55455
www.umn.edu

University of Nebraska
Fourteenth and R Sts.
Lincoln, NE 68588
www.unc.edu

University of North Carolina–Chapel Hill
Chapel Hill, NC 27599
www.unc.edu

University of Pennsylvania
Thirty-Fourth and Spruce St.
Philadelphia, PA 19104
www.upenn.edu

University of Toronto
100 St. George St.
Toronto, ON
Canada M5S 3G3
www.utstat.toronto.edu

University of Waterloo
200 University Ave. West
Waterloo, ON
Canada N2L 3G1
www.uwaterloo.ca

University of Western Ontario
London, ON
Canada N6A 5B7
www.uwo.ca

University of Wisconsin–Madison
500 Lincoln Dr.
Madison, WI 53706
wisc.edu

Appendix B

Licensing Agencies

Following is a list of state and provincial agencies to contact regarding licensing requirements.

United States

Alabama

Alabama Department of Insurance
201 Monroe St., Ste. 1700
Montgomery, AL 36104
www.aldoi.org

Alaska

Alaska Division of Insurance
550 W. 7th Ave., Ste. 1560
Anchorage, AK 99501-3567
www.commerce.state.ak.us/insurance

Arizona

Arizona Department of Insurance
2910 N. 44th St., Ste. 210
Phoenix, AZ 85018-7256
www.id.state.az.us

Arkansas

Arkansas Department of Insurance
1200 W. 3rd St.
Little Rock, AR 72201-1904
www.insurance.arkansas.gov/administration

California

California Department of Insurance
300 Capitol Mall, Ste. 1700
Sacramento, CA 95814
www.insurance.ca.gov

State of California
300 S. Spring St.
Los Angeles, CA 90013
www.dora.state.co.us/insurance

State of California
45 Fremont St., 23rd Fl.
San Francisco, CA 94105
www.insurance.ca.gov

Colorado

Colorado Division of Insurance
1560 Broadway, Ste. 850
Denver, CO 80202
www.dora.state.co.us/insurance

Connecticut

Connecticut Department of Insurance
P.O. Box 816
Hartford, CT 06142-0816
www.ct.gov/cid

Delaware

Delaware Department of Insurance
Rodney Bldg.
841 Silver Lake Blvd.
Dover, DE 19904
www.state.de.us/inscom

District of Columbia

Department of Insurance, Securities Regulation, and Banking
Government of the District of Columbia
810 First St. NE, Ste. 701
Washington, DC 20002
http://disr.washingtondc.gov/disr

Florida

Florida Department of Financial Services
200 E. Gaines St.
Tallahassee, FL 32399-0301
www.floir.com

Georgia

Georgia Department of Insurance
2 Martin Luther King Jr. Dr.
Floyd Memorial Bldg.
704 W. Tower
Atlanta, GA 30334
www.gainsurance.org

Hawaii

Hawaii Insurance Division
Department of Commerce and Consumer Affairs
P.O. Box 3614
Honolulu, HI 96811-3614
www.hawaii.gov/dcca

Idaho

Idaho Department of Insurance
700 W. State St., 3rd Fl.
Boise, ID 83720-0043
www.doi.idaho.gov

Illinois

Department of Financial and Professional Regulation
Illinois Division of Insurance
100 W. Randolph St., Ste. 9-301
Chicago, IL 60601-3251
www.idfpr.com

Indiana

Indiana Department of Insurance
311 W. Washington St., Ste. 300
Indianapolis, IN 46204-2787
www.ai.org/idoi

Iowa

Division of Insurance
State of Iowa
330 E. Maple St
Des Moines, IA 50319
www.iid.state.ia.us

Kansas

Kansas Department of Insurance
420 SW 9th St.
Topeka, KS 66612-1678
www.ksinsurance.org

Kentucky

Kentucky Office of Insurance
P.O. Box 517
Frankfort, KY 40602-0517
http://doi.ppr.ky.gov

Louisiana

Louisiana Department of Insurance
P.O. Box 94214
Baton Rouge, LA 70804-9214
www.ldi.state.la.us

Maine

Maine Bureau of Insurance
Department of Professional and Financial Regulation
State Office Bldg., Station 34
Augusta, ME 04333-0034
www.state.me.us/pfr/ins

Maryland

Maryland Insurance Administration
525 St. Paul Pl.
Baltimore, MD 21202-2272
www.mdinsurance.state.md.us

Massachusetts

Division of Insurance
Commonwealth of Massachusetts
One South Station, 5th Fl.
Boston, MA 02110
http://www.mass.gov

Michigan

Office of Financial and Insurance Services
Office of the Commissioner
P.O. Box 30220
Lansing, MI 48909
www.michigan.gov/cis

Minnesota

Minnesota Department of Commerce
85 7th Pl. E., Ste. 500
St. Paul, MN 55101-2198
www.state.mn.us

Mississippi

Mississippi Insurance Department
P.O. Box 79
Jackson, MS 39205
www.doi.state.ms.us

Missouri

Missouri Department of Insurance, Financial Institutions, and
  Professional Registration
301 W. High St., Ste. 530
Jefferson City, MO 65102
www.insurance.mo.gov

Montana

Montana Department of Insurance
840 Helena Ave.
Helena, MT 59601
http://sao.mt.gov

Nebraska

Nebraska Department of Insurance
Terminal Bldg., Ste. 400
941 "O" St.
Lincoln, NE 68508
www.doi.ne.gov

Nevada

Nevada Division of Insurance
788 Fairview Dr., Ste. 300
Carson City, NV 89701-5753
http://doi.state.nv.us

New Hampshire

New Hampshire Insurance Department
21 S. Fruit St., Ste. 14
Concord, NH 03301
www.nh.gov/insurance

New Jersey

New Jersey Department of Insurance
20 W. State St. CN325
Trenton, NJ 08625
www.state.nj.us/dobi

New Mexico

New Mexico Insurance Division
P.O. Drawer 1269
Santa Fe, NM 87504-1269
www.nmprc.state.nm.us

New York

New York Department of Insurance
One Commerce Plaza, Ste. 1700
Albany, NY 12257
www.ins.state.ny.us

New York Department of Insurance
25 Beaver St.
New York, NY 10004-2319
www.ins.state.ny.us

North Carolina

North Carolina Department of Insurance
1201 Mail Service Ctr.
Raleigh, NC 27699-1201
www.ncdoi.com

North Dakota

North Dakota Department of Insurance
600 E. Blvd.
Bismarck, ND 58505-0320
www.nd.gov/ndins

Ohio

Ohio Department of Insurance
2100 Stella Ct.
Columbus, OH 43215-1067
www.ohioinsurance.gov

Oklahoma

Oklahoma Department of Insurance
2401 NW 23rd St., Ste. 28
Oklahoma City, OK 73107
www.oid.state.ok.us

Oregon

Oregon Insurance Division
P.O. Box 14480
Salem, OR 97309-0405
www.cbs.state.or.us/external/ins

Pennsylvania

Pennsylvania Insurance Department
1326 Strawberry Sq., 13th Fl.
Harrisburg, PA 17120
www.ins.state.pa.us/ins

Rhode Island

Rhode Island Insurance Division
Department of Business Regulation
233 Richmond St., Ste. 233
Providence, RI 02903-4233
www.dbr.state.ri.us

South Carolina

South Carolina Department of Insurance
P.O. Box 100105
Columbia, SC 29202-3105
www.doi.sc.gov

South Dakota

South Dakota Division of Insurance
Department of Revenue and Regulation
445 E. Capitol Ave., 1st Fl.
Pierre, SD 57501-3185
www.state.sd.us

Tennessee

Tennessee Department of Commerce and Insurance
Davy Crockett Tower, 5th Fl.
500 James Robertson Pkwy.
Nashville, TN 37243-0565
www.state.tn.us/commerce/insurance

Texas

Texas Department of Insurance
P.O. Box 149104
Austin, TX 78714-9104
www.state.tn.us/commerce/insurance

Utah

Utah Department of Insurance
3110 State Office Bldg.
Salt Lake City, UT 84114-1201
www.insurance.utah.gov

Vermont

Vermont Division of Insurance
Department of Banking, Insurance, and Securities
89 Main St., Drawer 20
Montpelier, VT 05620-3101
www.bishca.state.vt.us

Virginia

State Corporation Commission, Bureau of Insurance
Commonwealth of Virginia
P.O. Box 1157
Richmond, VA 23218
www.scc.virginia.gov/division/boi

Washington

Washington State Office of the Insurance Commissioner
P.O. Box 40255
Olympia, WA 98504-0255
www.insurance.wa.gov

West Virginia

West Virginia Department of Insurance
P.O. Box 50540
Charleston, WV 25305-0540
www.wvinsurance.gov

Wisconsin

Office of the Commissioner of Insurance
State of Wisconsin
P.O. Box 7873
Madison, WI 53707-7873
http://oci.wi.gov

Wyoming

Wyoming Department of Insurance
Herschler Bldg.
122 W. 25th St., 3rd E.
Cheyenne, WY 82002-0440
http://insurance.state.wy.us

Canada

Alberta

Alberta Insurance Council
Toronto Dominion Tower
901-10088 102 Ave.
Edmonton, AB
Canada T5J 2Z1
www.abcouncil.ab.ca

British Columbia

Insurance Council of British Columbia
300-1040 W. Georgia
P.O. Box 7
Vancouver, BC
Canada V6E 4H1
www.insurancecouncilofbc.com

Manitoba

Insurance Council of Manitoba
466-167 Lombard Ave.
Winnipeg, MB
Canada R3B 0T6
www.icm.mb.ca

New Brunswick

Insurance Branch, Dept. of Justice
175-670 King St., Centennial Bldg.
P.O. Box 6000
Fredericton, NB
Canada E3B 5H1
www.gnb.ca

Newfoundland and Labrador

Dept. of Government Services and Lands
Confederation Bldg., 2nd Fl., West Block
Prince Philip Dr.
P.O. Box 8700
St. John's, NF
Canada A1B 4J6
www.gov.nf.ca

Northwest Territories and Nunavut

Dept. of Finance
Treasury Division, Government of the Northwest Territories
P.O. Box 1320
Yellowknife, NT
Canada X1A 2L9
www.fin.gov.nt.ca

Nova Scotia

Dept. of Environment and Labour
Financial Institutions Division
5151 Terminal Rd., 7th Fl.
Halifax, NS
Canada B3J 1A1
www.gov.ns.ca/enla

Ontario

Financial Services Commission of Ontario
5160 Yonge St., 17th Fl., Box 85
North York, ON
Canada M2N 6L9
www.fsco.gov.on.ca

Registered Insurance Brokers of Ontario
1200-401 Bay St., Box 45
Toronto, ON
Canada M5H 2Y4
www.ribo.com

Prince Edward Island

Dept. of Community Services and Office of the Attorney General
95 Rochford St.
Charlottetown, PE
Canada C1A 7N8
www.gov.pe.ca

Québec

Autorité des marches financiers
Place de la Cité, Tour Cominar
2640 Blvd. Laurier, Bureau 400
Sainte-Foy, QC
Canada G1V 5C1
www.lautorite.qc.ca

Chambre de l'assurance de dommages
500, rue Sherbrooke Ouest, 7 étage
Montréal, QC
Canada H3A 3C6
www.chad.qc.ca

Saskatchewan

Insurance Council of Saskatchewan
310-2631 28th Ave.
Regina, SK
Canada S4S 6X3
www.bas.sk.ca

Yukon

Consumer Service J-6
Government of Yukon
P.O. Box 2703
Whitehorse, YK
Canada Y1A 2C6
www.gov.yk.ca

Glossary

Actual cash value The amount of money a policyholder can expect to recover under the terms of most property insurance policies for damage to or destruction of property. This is subject to the maximum limit of insurance stated in the contract and all other restrictions or requirements within the contract. This amount is what it would take to replace the property at the time of loss, after making a fair deduction for depreciation due to wear and tear, obsolescence, or for the degree to which the property has lost its usefulness.

Actual total loss A type of loss used in marine insurance. If a casualty from insured perils has made it impossible for the insured property to reach its destination, an actual total loss has been suffered. For a contrasting term, see "Constructive total loss."

Actuary An expert in the field of insurance mathematics and statistics who deals primarily with problems in the science of rate making.

Adhesion, contract of An insurance contract prepared by one party, without significant negotiation with the second party, which the second party must essentially accept or reject as is. In cases of ambiguity, a court will lean in favor of the party that did not prepare the contract.

Adjuster A person who investigates and settles claims for losses incurred under property and casualty policies.

Adjustment Refers to all of the steps involved in an adjuster's work in settling a claim against an insurer, including investigations, the determination of loss amounts, and settlement agreement.

Agency relationship The relationship that exists between the agent and the agent's principal. An agency relationship should be of the utmost good faith, especially when insurance is involved.

Agent One who acts for another. In insurance, the term usually refers to a local agent or a general agent. A local agent acts mainly as a sales and service representative for a company. The local agent has somewhat limited authority, even though he or she is an independent contractor. A general agent supervises company operations within a specified area and has broad managerial powers.

Alien company An insurance company organized outside the United States. See "Domestic company" and "Foreign company" for contrasting terms.

All risk coverage A type of insurance policy that protects the insured against loss from any and all perils except those that are specifically listed by the contract as excluded.

Application A printed form, usually in the nature of a statement or questionnaire, that must be completed by the prospective insured to provide the underwriter with sufficient information to decide whether the risk submitted for insurance is acceptable.

Appraisal clause A provision in property insurance contracts giving the insurance company and the insured the right to demand an appraisal of the damage by an impartial group of experts. This occurs in the event of failure to come to agreement over the amount of damage to property covered by the policy.

Assessment clause A provision found in the insurance policies of some mutual insurers and reciprocal exchanges stating the amount that member policyholders may be called upon to pay if total losses of the company over a given period of time exceed funds available to cover the payment. In numerous instances, such assessments are limited by policy terms to one extra annual premium deposit per policyholder.

Assumption of risk A defense to a charge of negligence, such as an injured person voluntarily and with knowledge deciding to do something that places her or him at risk. It was also one of the common law defenses used by employers before the advent of workers' compensation laws.

Attorney-in-fact An individual given legal authority to act for another, generally by means of a contract known as a *power of attorney*. In insurance, the manager of a reciprocal exchange is an attorney-in-fact, given power to carry on the daily management and other activities of the exchange.

Average A term used in marine insurance law to mean partial loss. A general average is a partial loss that generally falls on all the interests at risk in a maritime venture. This loss occurs when some of the property at risk is sacrificed to save the remainder. A particular average is a partial loss that falls on one interest, because it is not due to the type of sacrifice to which the law of general average applies.

Aviation insurance Insurance involving activities having to do with aviation, such as coverage of the aircraft and liability for injury and property damage in the air and on the ground.

Binder A written agreement that is used when a policy cannot be issued immediately. The terms of a binder are generally thought of as the same as the policy that will replace the binder, unless otherwise stated.

Blanket form A form of contract that provides coverage for similar types of property located at different locations or may provide coverage for different types of property at the same location. It also provides coverage for all employees or for a class of employees without their being individually named.

Broad form A form of contract. Generally, it adds additional perils to the standard form of a policy. The perils added may vary, depending on the type of insurance concerned.

Broker A type of salesperson. According to the usual understanding, a broker does not represent a company but rather represents the client. He or she may write insurance in a number of companies.

Bureau, rating An organization that gathers loss statistics and other pertinent information essential for rate-making purposes. The rating bureau computes and classifies rates from such data for filing with the state insurance authorities on behalf of its subscribers and member companies.

Business interruption The most common type of insurance for consequential or indirect losses from fire. It pays for a loss of business income when a fire destroys the building in which a business is operating.

Cancellation The policy provision that permits the insurance company to terminate coverage before the end of the policy period. Cancellation provisions are always set forth in the policy.

Claim A request for payment due to loss under a policy of insurance covering the type of loss sustained.

Co-insurance The division of the risk between the insurer and the insured.

Commissioner of insurance A state official normally charged with the duties of regulating insurance company activities in the public interest and administering insurance laws.

Comparative negligence Under these laws, the jury or court decides on the comparative degree of negligence involving the plaintiff and defendant and decides damages to be paid on that basis.

Condition A future and uncertain event upon whose happening depends the existence of an obligation in a contract.

Consequential damage or loss Such damage, loss, or injury as does not flow directly and immediately from the act of the party, but only from some of the consequences or results of such act. In an insurance context, a consequential loss is one that results as the consequence of an event that results in a loss.

Consideration One of the four required elements in the formation of an informal contract. Both parties must give up something of value in order to form the contract.

Constructive total loss In marine insurance, constructive total loss occurs when it is still possible for the property to reach its destination, but the cost of getting it there would exceed the value of the property. Thus, the insured notifies the insurance underwriter of the decision to abandon all rights to the property.

Contributory negligence A defense to a charge of negligence. Contributory negligence is conduct by the plaintiff that contributed (as a legal cause) to the harm the plaintiff has suffered; this conduct falls below the standard to which the plaintiff is required to conform for her or his own protection. It was also one of the common law defenses available to employers of injured workers before the advent of workers' compensation laws.

Cooperation clause Found in liability policies, providing that upon the insurer's request, the insured shall attend hearings and trials and shall assist in affecting settlements, securing and giving evidence, obtaining the attendance of witnesses, and conducting suits.

Declarations The page inside the cover of many policies, usually typed or machine printed, providing identifying information concerning the insured, the insured property, and applicable coverages.

Deductible An amount of money that the insured pays and the insurance company does not. Frequently, it is the first part of a claim amount, after which the insurance company begins paying under the claim.

Direct loss Direct damage to an insured property or person as a result of a loss that is insured against.

Direct-writing company A classification of insurance companies according to their marketing approaches. These are companies that sell insurance by means of their own sales force.

Disability benefit A cash sum paid periodically, such as weekly or monthly, on account of the disability of the insured. Such benefits are paid under automobile and other types of insurance, as well as under workers' compensation provisions.

Dividend In a mutual company, unused portions of the premiums paid by policyholders, returned to them periodically as a savings, after all company loss and operating expenses have been met and something has been added to the surplus fund account. In a stock company, a dividend is that portion of income (earnings) in excess of losses and expenses, distributed to stockholders as a return on their invested capital.

Domestic company A classification of insurance companies according to the location of the home office. It is a company organized in the state to which an individual is referring

Earned premium That portion of any policy premium that would pay the cost of protection provided by the company up to the present moment.

Endorsement A form printed and attached to an insurance policy, usually in order to add something to it, take something from it, or otherwise modify or change the policy.

Exclusions Those provisions of a policy that describe types of property, perils, hazards, or other items for which there is no coverage.

Experience Generally, the total loss record of a company for a given period or the actual loss record on particular classes of insurance for such a period.

Experience rating A rating device for comparing the loss record of a particular risk with the average loss record of all other risks of the same general class.

Exposure A term expressing the fact that something is subject to possible loss from some peril or hazard. For example, a home exposed to gasoline tanks could be said to have a severe exposure to the perils of fire or explosions.

Extended coverage An endorsement or section of one of the standard insurance forms usually attached to a basic fire insurance policy to extend it for coverage of such perils as windstorms, hail, and explosions.

Federal crime insurance Insurance provided to insure against burglary, robbery, and other theft against property and persons. It was enacted because of the difficulty encountered by property owners in obtaining commercial coverage in areas where the crime rate was expected to be high.

Federal flood insurance Insurance provided to make coverage available in areas that experience a high incidence of flooding and where commercial companies are unable to provide coverage at an affordable premium.

Federal riot insurance Designed to provide property insurance for policyholders who live in areas that are particularly susceptible to potential riot damage and who cannot purchase coverage from commercial companies.

Fidelity bond A contract under which any losses sustained by an employer due to the dishonesty of an employee covered by the contract are made good by the insurance company as surety.

Fire-resistive Referring to a type of property judged by strict engineering standards as having an unusual capacity to resist fire. This term is used in insurance circles as a preference to the more popularly used term *fireproof*, because there is not actually a type of property that is not subject to damage by fire.

Floater policy A form often used synonymously with inland marine policies but more accurately defined as a policy covering property in the course of transportation, wherever it may be moved. Such policies frequently cover the same property on the premises where it is normally located.

Foreign company A classification of an insurance company according to the location of the home office. A foreign company is one organized in another state of the United States.

Hazard A condition of circumstances increasing the likelihood that loss will occur.

Homeowner's policy A package policy combining property insurance with liability coverage. Coverage is integrated with fixed relationships among the coverages, with a single premium applying to the whole package.

Indemnity Compensation for damage, loss, or injury incurred. Property and casualty insurance policies are usually contracts of indemnity that reimburse for the amount of loss rather than pay a particular amount without regard for the amount of loss. The latter type of contract is a valued contract.

Inland marine insurance Insurance that is provided to take care of property while it is on land during transit. Its major types of coverage include transportation policies, bailee insurance, and personal property coverage.

Inspection A report used in underwriting. Inspection consists of checking public information, such as traffic report records and financial filings, and interviewing persons likely to have pertinent information concerning the proposed insured and her or his business operation.

Insurable risk A risk that has the characteristics that make it insurable. The characteristics include that it must be susceptible to the law of large numbers, the occurrences of loss must be uncertain, the loss must be of a nature to cause significant difficulty, losses must be irregular in occurrence, the cost of insuring the risk must be low in comparison to the coverage itself, and the risk must be determinable.

Insurance A contract by which one party, for a compensation called the *premium*, assumes particular risks of the other party and promises to pay to her or him, or to her or his nominee, a certain or ascertainable sum of money on a specified contingency.

Insuring clauses Clauses, usually printed in the policy, that set forth the consideration being provided, the specifics of what is being insured, the promise to pay the amount of damages agreed on, and similar provisions.

Interinsurance company Also called the *reciprocal*; this is a system under which several individuals may underwrite each other's risks against various hazards through an attorney-in-fact common to all, under an agreement that each underwriter acts separately for one another.

Lapse A situation in which an insurance policy has automatically ceased to remain in force beyond a specified date because of the policyholder's failure to pay a premium.

Liability insurance Insurance providing protection for a person's legal responsibility for acts that result in injuries to other persons or damages to other persons' property.

Licensing The procedure for applying for, qualifying for, and issuing a license to carry on an insurance activity.

Limit of liability The maximum amount the insurance company is obligated to pay under the coverage. Generally, liability limits are different for different coverage within one policy.

Lloyd's organization A type of insurer, the best known being Lloyd's of London. Each member of a Lloyd's organization is an individual insurer.

Loss ratio The proportion of the premiums received by the insurer that are paid out in losses. If more is paid out than is taken in, rates are not adequate.

Malpractice insurance A type of liability insurance that insures against legal liability on account of improper or negligent treatment or procedures by the insured or a person under the direction of the insured.

Manual rating The most common type of rating done. Risks that are similar are charged a rate contained in the manual of rates, since they are likely to produce similar loss results.

McCarran-Ferguson Act The federal law that states that the regulation of the business of insurance shall remain a matter of state control except in those areas where Congress has declared otherwise with specific legislation.

Misrepresentation A deliberate misstatement of a material fact about the proposed subject matter of insurance, fraudulently made by an applicant to persuade the underwriter to cover a risk that the underwriter would not have covered if he or she had known the facts.

Named peril policy The type of policy that lists the particular perils covered. Any unnamed perils are excluded, or not covered.

National Association of Insurance Commissioners (NAIC) The association of state insurance department heads. The organization meets to exchange ideas, discuss matters of mutual interest, and formulate model legislative bills having to do with insurance.

Negligence The omission of something that a reasonable person, guided by those ordinary considerations that regulate human affairs, would do or the doing of something that a reasonable and prudent person would not do.

No-fault automobile insurance An approach to automobile insurance where everyone who is injured, either bodily or by damage to property, can first recover from her or his own insurance company without resorting to legal action. More serious or costly damages can be recovered through legal action.

Non-participating insurance This is insurance issued by stock companies that are said not to participate in the earnings of the company, since no policy dividends are payable from the company's surplus.

Notice of loss The provision in a policy calling for the notification of the insurer and a later filing of appropriate proof in the event of a loss covered by the policy.

Obligee A term used with bonds. It is the person to whom the surety's promise is made on behalf of the principal.

Ocean marine insurance Types of insurance involving transportation of goods over oceans and similar bodies of water.

Partial disability A term used in workers' compensation. Partial disability impairs earning ability but does not involve a total inability to work. It may be required that partial disability follow a period of total disability in order that compensation be payable.

Participating insurance Insurance issued by mutual companies and, in some instances, by stock companies that participate in the earnings of the company in that dividends are payable to the policyholder from the surplus of the company.

Paul v. Virginia The case, decided by the United States Supreme Court in 1868, that held that the business of insurance was not commerce.

Peril The risk, hazard, or contingency insured against by a policy of insurance. Peril also states the possible cause of loss. Fire and hail are perils, for example.

Premium The payment, or one of the periodic payments, a policyholder agrees to make for an insurance policy.

Principal A term used with bonds. The surety agrees to compensate the obligee, on behalf of the principal, if the principal does not perform as agreed. The principal is the one who is to do the performing.

Proof of loss Part of the provisions in the policy having to do with notice of loss and providing information. The proof is the evidence as to the loss itself.

Protection In general, the total coverage provided by an insurance policy.

Proximate cause That which, in a natural and continuous sequence, produces injury and without which the resultant injury would not have occurred.

Rate-making The process of establishing a rate that is correct for the risk. Principles involved are non-discrimination, rate adequacy, economic practicality, rate moderateness, and non-fluctuation in rates.

Real property land or real estate Other property is personal property. Generally, real property includes the buildings located on it and fixtures affixed to the buildings.

Reasonable person The fictitious person who serves as the standard for deciding whether the defendant has acted in a negligent fashion.

Representation An oral or written statement by the insured to the insurer, made prior to the completion of the contract, giving information as to some fact with respect to the subject of the insurance.

Reserve The measure of the funds that an insurance company holds specifically for fulfillment of its policy obligations. Methods of calculating reserves are prescribed by law.

Retrospective rating A type of rate-making based on the insured's own loss experience, where the insured and insurer negotiate a minimum and maximum premium for the year. The premium eventually paid, usually between the maximum and minimum, is based on experience.

Risk The danger or hazard of loss of the insured's property. Generally, risk is indicated and calculated as a percentage, with the percentage having to do with the probability of loss.

Safe driving plan Private passenger automobile insurance rates are based on the individual's driving record and those of other drivers who reside with the insured. Not only are convictions for traffic offenses taken into account but also accidents where the insured or another driver was not at fault.

Salvage A term used with bonds. It is the amount recovered from the employee who is the subject of a fidelity bond. The contract determines which party of the contract will receive the salvage.

Schedule form A policy form that lists separate items at several locations. Each item of personal property or building is specifically described, but all are covered by the same form, with the amount of coverage on each item being the proportionate share of the total amount of all items.

Schedule rating A type of rating applicable when the insured has undertaken loss prevention techniques. The insured provides a schedule indicating loss prevention measures; these products rate deviations.

Self-insurance When self-funding an insurance plan, an employer assumes the risk normally passed on to the insurance company. This is done in an effort to control costs, save money, and gain internal control of an insurance plan.

Southeastern Underwriters v. United States The case, decided by the United States Supreme Court in 1944, that held that the business of insurance is interstate commerce.

Standard fire insurance policy The commonly used and standardized policy used for fire insurance coverage on buildings. It is frequently enhanced by extended coverage.

Stock company A classification of insurance companies by the way they are organized. A stock company is one in which an initial capital investment is made by the subscribers to the stock, and the business is thereafter conducted by a board of directors elected by the stockholders. The distribution of earnings or profits is determined by the board of directors.

Strict liability Liability without the necessity of establishing that the defendant is at fault. It is generally found in cases where dangerous materials are in use.

Subsequent injury A term used with workers' compensation. An injury sustained by an employee who has suffered a previous injury, such that the disability resulting from the effect of the combined injuries is greater than would be due to the second injury alone.

Superseded suretyship A rider attached to a fidelity bond that provides that any loss occurring under the prior bond, which would have been paid if that bond had continued in force, will be paid by the new bond.

Surety A term used with bonds. Surety is the person (frequently with an insurance company) who makes good the promise of the principal to the obligee.

Surety bond A contract under which a person (surety) agrees to perform on behalf of the principal that has been promised the obligee. It covers the financial strength of the covered person, the person's honesty, her or his ability, or a combination of these.

Tenants' form A form of the homeowners' policy applicable to those who rent the dwelling. Essentially all of the coverages of the homeowners' package are included in this form, except those applying to the dwelling.

Term insurance A life insurance policy that is to remain in force over a relatively short period for the purpose of protecting the beneficiary named against premature death of the insured.

Theft insurance Coverage against various forms of theft. Many theft policies pertain to only some of the forms of theft, while others pertain to nearly all forms.

Time limits provisions Provisions in policies that impose limitations as to when claims must be submitted and proofs of loss submitted, how soon lawsuits may be started, and how long after a loss a suit may be brought.

Tort Any wrongful act, damage, or injury done willfully, negligently, or in circumstances involving strict liability, but not involving breach of contract, for which a civil suit can be brought.

Transportation insurance Coverage for instrumentalities of transportation and the goods being transported. It is a type of inland marine insurance. Policies cover either the property itself or the acts of the insured, the insured's employee, or the insured's agent.

Unearned premium The part of the original premium charged for the insurance that cannot be considered "earned" by the company beyond the current date, since protection still must be provided throughout the remaining life of the contract.

Uninsured motorists' insurance Insurance that provides for payment to the insured for damages to which he or she is entitled because of bodily injury, sickness, or disease caused by the owner or operator of an uninsured automobile.

Valued contract A type of insurance contract. It pays the insured or the insured's beneficiary a certain amount or value regardless of the loss incurred.

Vicarious liability laws These laws hold the owner of a car or other vehicle responsible for liability arising from the use of the vehicle by another person so long as the person using it is driving with the permission of the owner.

Waiting period A term used with disability income as provided under workers' compensation, automobile insurance, and health insurance. It is the period that must elapse, following the onset of disability, before payments under the policy begin.

Waiver A voluntary and intentional relinquishment of a known and existing right. The term is applied when a party, usually by its conduct, acts in such a way as to abandon a requirement that would otherwise be necessary.

Warranty A statement on the part of the insurer, frequently appearing in the policy or in another instrument incorporated into the policy, relating to the risk insured against. A warranty is a part of the contract.

Workers' compensation Statutes that brought forth the idea of strict liability on the part of employers for the injuries of employees while they were at work. The costs of compensation are considered legitimate costs of production, which should be shifted to the consumer as part of the cost of the goods produced.

About the Author

ROBERT M. SCHRAYER was born in Chicago, Illinois. He attended Kenwood Grammar School, the University of Chicago Lab School, and Harvard High School before matriculating to the University of Michigan at Ann Arbor, where he received a Bachelor of Arts degree in philosophy in 1954.

Following his graduation from the University of Michigan, he entered the insurance industry as an employee of The Associated Agencies, Inc., in Chicago. He later attended the Insurance Company of North America's School for Agents in Pennsylvania to acquire specific insurance skills. Through the years, he assumed invaluable experience in the field and eventually became vice president and part owner of the insurance agency.

In 1971 Schrayer left Associated Agencies, Inc., to form his own insurance agency, Robert M. Schrayer Company. In 1986 his company purchased The Associated Agencies, Inc., and assumed operations under the banner of Associated Agencies, Inc.

This edition was revised by Mark Rowh, a professional career book author and vice president of planning and advancement at New River Community College in Dublin, Virginia.